Trustworthy Government

Trustworthy Government

Leadership and Management Strategies for Building Trust and High Performance

David G. Carnevale

Jossey-Bass Publishers • San Francisco

Substantial discounts on bulk quantities of Jossey-Bass books are available to corporations, professional associations, and other organizations. For details and discount information, contact the special sales department at Jossey-Bass Inc., Publishers. (415) 433-1740; Fax (800) 605-2665.

For sales outside the United States, please contact your local Paramount Publishing International office.

Manufactured in the United States of America on Lyons Falls Pathfinder Tradebook. TCF This paper is acid-free and 100 percent totally chlorine-free.

Library of Congress Cataloging-in-Publication Data

Carnevale, David G., date.
    Trustworthy government : leadership and management strategies for building trust and high performance / David G. Carnevale. — 1st ed.
        p.   cm. — (The Jossey-Bass public administration series)
    Includes bibliographical references and index.
    ISBN 0-7879-0062-1
    1. Public administration—United States—Management. 2. Leadership. I. Title.
II. Series.
JF1351.C3526   1995
350.007—dc20   94-38540

HB Printing   10 9 8 7 6 5 4 3 2 1   FIRST EDITION

The Jossey-Bass Public Administration Series

Consulting Editor
Public Management and Administration

James L. Perry
Indiana University

To Karen, Kelly, Katie, and Kim

Contents

PART THREE
Liberating Public Organizations: Transcending the Bureaucratic Machine

Preface

Trust is an expression of faith and confidence that a person or an institution will be fair, reliable, ethical, competent, and nonthreatening. In the world of work, there is a pervasive "trust gap," and it is widening. Many Americans go to their jobs with guarded, suspicious, and cynical attitudes. They have lost faith in their organizations. Their hopes and expectations have been mismanaged. The costs of mistrust and cynicism are high. These emotions corrode organizations and destroy high performance. The loss of trust is a loss of system power in organizations. Trust is an integrative mechanism—the cohesion that makes it possible for organizations to accomplish extraordinary things. Trust is social capital. It reduces conflict, improves communication, eases cooperation, enhances problem solving, reduces stress, enables people to realize more satisfactory relationships, amplifies organizational learning, and advances change. Trust is a positive mindset. It needs to be restored in organizations.

Trust and Learning

The core performance advantage in every organization is how the capacity of its knowledge base is established and used. In high-performing systems, learning is enabled, liberated, and used to gain competitive advantage. In low-trust work cultures, learning potential is systematically repressed and destroyed in two ways. First, mistrustful people engage in defensive, self-protective behaviors. Because of their wary posture, they cannot learn effectively. They are not as open to the influence of others or are just plain fearful of disclosing what they know. The sharing of information—the key to learning—is stifled. Second, low-trust work cultures typically feature authoritarian command, an obsession with control, and impoverished, low-discretion work roles. Creative energy is crushed in such climates. In contemporary organizations, where the emancipation of knowledge is the crucial technology, the result is devastating.

Audience

People concerned with management, organizational behavior, personnel administration, and labor relations will find *Trustworthy Government* indispensable for understanding one of the most meaningful and least understood variables in organizational life. The book is written principally for people interested in government institutions. However, the fundamental precepts are equally valuable to individuals—both practitioners and academics—with concerns outside the public sector. The core principles will travel well across a broad range of organization types, no matter where they are nested.

The critical topics of leadership, motivation, participation, communication, power, politics, and conflict all receive serious attention. Human resources management and the transition it must make for success in modern organizations are covered in-depth.

Purpose

The primary goal of the book is to help people comprehend what trust is all about and why it is absolutely vital in organizations. Leaders influence the level of trust in their organization by the way they manage work roles, rules, and relations. Levels of trust, in turn, influence individual learning and organizational accomplishment. If the book does what I expect, people will recognize themselves, their co-workers, and their organizations in its pages. They will also see what needs to be done to improve trust in public institutions. The tone is somewhat passionate and critical, but that is necessary and appropriate given both the nature of the topic and the realities about levels of trust in contemporary organizations. However, I have always been optimistic at heart about what is possible for people at work, and I hope that shows through.

Origins

The genesis of the book arises from my experiences as an employee, public union representative, graduate student, and teacher. I suppose it is true that the questions that we ask and the topics that attract us are driven by our biographies. Throughout my graduate education I kept running into the subject of trust, and my work experience reinforced its importance. While it received lots of notice in the popular and scholarly literature, I could find no comprehensive model of its determinants and effects. So I set out to create a model.

The model of trust that I developed included both individual and organizational predictors. Test results showed that people's feelings of trust are most influenced by how organizations arrange and administer key work processes, particularly (1) opportunities to participate, (2) open communications, (3) fairness in the administration of rewards and punishments, (4) enriched job design, and (5) flexible supervision. I concluded that democratic—rather than bureaucratic—organizations build higher levels of trust. Since the initial study of several thousand state employees in Florida, my research on learning and dispute resolution has reinforced and extended earlier insights and furthered my appreciation of how trust operates and why it is so consequential.

Overview

Part One introduces the subject of trust, indicates the state of trust in public institutions, shows why the topic is especially meaningful today, and explains how the legacy of management practices introduced at the turn of the century continue to impair trust in organizations.

Chapter One examines the topic by defining trust and

establishing its myriad relationships to various organizational processes. The crisis of trust in organizations is described and the sources of this crisis are revealed.

Chapter Two shows how trust operates. Trust is a reciprocal attitude—people tend to reflect the amount of trust that is directed toward them. This means that how organizations are structured and managed communicates how much employees are trusted. Staff members understand the unspoken messages in an organization's structure and respond in kind. The implication is straightforward: Trust begets trust. The opposite is also true. The connection between trust, learning, and high performance—the core theory of this book—is established. Simply put, people cannot learn, nor are they willing to reveal what they know, when they are cynical, suspicious, or fearful. Repressing people's knowhow short-circuits high performance.

Chapter Three underscores the importance of employee commitment as the chief basis for superior achievement in organizations. The difference between simple compliance and "beyond-contract" or higher-order involvement is illustrated. High-performance organizations need people who do more than what is expected. No organization reaches high performance without strong staff commitment.

An important point in this chapter is that everyone matters in organizations. The book eschews an "us versus them" stance, where front-line personnel are seen as the only ones who count when it comes to organizational accomplishment. In all the recent enthusiasm for empowering employees down the line, the still important role of supervisors and managers is receiving insufficient attention. The knowledge of *all* employees contributes to high performance. Therefore, creating mistrust among managers is as poisonous as fostering cynicism on the front line. This chapter also provides a critique of traditional motivational techniques. The point is that motivational plans have their place in fostering trust only as long as they are not manipulative. People need to feel good on the job, but that by itself is not sufficient. They also need more control and power over their work. Motivational schemes that aim to change simply how people feel, but not their working conditions, are doomed to fail. Much more is necessary to create trust in postmodern work systems.

Part Two shifts the discussion to other key organizational processes that require attention in building institutionalized systems of trust.

Chapter Four focuses on leadership. The quality of leadership is vital in organizations, but it's also true that too many people overestimate leadership's importance in conditioning beliefs about trust. In fact, leadership—like motivation—can actually backfire and cause mistrust under certain circumstances. The relationship of trust to leadership is discussed and an assessment of highly personalized leadership styles is provided. This chapter covers both the positive and negative aspects of charismatic leadership approaches. The discussion then moves to substitutes for leadership and how they can support trust and learning. The message is that people have to rely on their own knowledge, skills, and abilities and master effective self-management strategies to realize superior achievement over the long haul. It is in themselves that people must ultimately place their trust. Superior leaders diffuse authority throughout their organizations. They teach people to lead themselves.

Chapter Five reviews the importance of participative processes for creating trust, cooperation, and high performance. Participation elevates feelings of personal efficacy by granting staff more control over their work lives. Involving employees means trusting them with information, power, authority, and responsibility. They interpret their enhanced control over the conception and execution of their work as expressions of confidence, and they respond accordingly. This chapter argues that enriched and empowering work roles increase trust, learning, and performance. The special problems associated with boosting levels of participation in public organizations are outlined.

Chapter Six explains the necessity of open communications as a precursor of trust and learning. Both depend on the free flow of intelligence in social systems. The problem of valuable information being driven underground, particularly in hierarchical authority structures, is considered. Overcoming barriers to open communications is then addressed.

Chapter Seven deals with the importance of fairness in the administration of rewards and punishments as a precondition for trust. It does little good to create high-powered learning systems only to have them undercut by misused organizational incentive structures. This chapter revisits motivational theories, especially expectancy and equity concepts, and discusses how they affect trust relations at work. The association between fair administration of organizational incentive systems and equitable performance appraisal methods is confirmed. Finally, the chapter shows why procedural due process, high-input process control, and alternative dispute-resolution mechanisms are so pivotal in establishing feelings of trust. People trust outcomes more when they have a hand in fashioning them.

Chapter Eight depicts how the management of power, politics, and conflict affects trust. The essential point is that these dynamics are natural in organizations. It is not a matter of whether these energies will exist, but what form they will take. This chapter portrays different sources of power, along with their strengths and weaknesses for creating conditions of trust and learning. It then illuminates how conflict can be constructively handled and how politics can be ethically directed.

Part Three shows how human resources management techniques must change to support trust-building activities and why democratic governance systems are more friendly to trust. The theme in the last three chapters is that traditional, bureaucratic approaches to administration must be altered to realize higher states of trust, learning, and high performance in organizations.

Chapter Nine is concerned with the importance and development of human capital. Human resources development is one of the most important trust-building enterprises in organizations.

What is called for is the application of a radically different learning theory at work, one that relies on critical self-reflection rather than traditional behavioral training. The difference between supply-side and demand-side strategies in the creation of organizational learning systems is explained. Finally, the state of human capital development in the public sector is discussed.

Chapter Ten deals specifically with human resources management challenges in modern organizations. A traditional model of human resources administration is compared with an alternative learning support model with respect to organizational arrangements, institutional roles, job design, compensation plans, organizational learning, and labor relations. Much of what passes for management innovation these days coexists with personnel systems with underlying ideas that have not changed much since the beginning of the century. Unless human resources management is strategically in synch with modern management philosophy and practice, programs to improve organizational performance cannot succeed.

The book concludes with a summary of the central themes and connects them with the components of democratic work organizations. The problems of establishing democracy within administration are discussed and summary principles to achieve trust, learning, and high performance are presented.

Acknowledgments

I am indebted to a number of people for the ideas incorporated here. I owe debts to those people who have taught me about people and work: P. J. Ciampa, Peter Damborg, Steve Fantauzzo, John Marvin, Mike Miller, John Oliver, Jerry Wurf, and literally thousands of public employees that I have had the privilege to represent. I also wish to thank the faculty at Florida State University who helped focus my thinking about people in organizations, particularly Jim Bowman, Richard Chackerian, Hal Rainey, Frank Sherwood, and Bart Wechsler. As always, my deep gratitude to my brothers Tony and John. Special thanks goes to my good friend and colleague Ralph Hummel, who kept encouraging me to hammer away. To my students who evaluated chapters goes much appreciation, especially Steve Housel, Jo Rios, and Kathy Sheegog. I am grateful to Alan Shrader at Jossey-Bass and to James Perry for their support of this project and their helpful comments, which have improved it immensely. Noelle Graney at Jossey-Bass improved the book as well. I would also like to express my gratitude to Catherine Blaha and Menah Moses, who worked very hard to help produce this manuscript. To my family—Karen, Kelly, Katie, and Kim—much love for tolerating and understanding the stresses that authorship creates.

Norman, Oklahoma   David G. Carnevale
January 1995

The Author

David G. Carnevale is a member of the political science department at the University of Oklahoma, where he is also director, Programs in Public Administration. He received his B.A. degree (1969) in political science from the University of Maine in Portland, and his Ph.D. degree (1989) in public administration from Florida State University.

Carnevale's principal research activities have been in the areas of human capital development, labor-management cooperation, and physical conditions of work. He has published articles in a number of scholarly journals, such as *Public Administration Review*, *Administration and Society*, *American Review of Public Administration*, and *Public Productivity and Management Review*. He has also contributed book chapters on staff training and development, recruitment of public employees, and municipal management.

Carnevale was executive director of the Maine State Employees Association from 1970 to 1975, operations administrator of the California State Employees Association from 1976 to 1981, and international union area director for AFSCME, AFL-CIO, from 1981 to 1985. He has consulted with and conducted conflict-resolution training for several public organizations.

Trustworthy Government

PART ONE

Trust: The Hidden Ingredient in High Performance

1

The Crisis of Trust in Today's Organizations

American government is facing a crisis of approval, credibility, and legitimacy. People are cynical about the effectiveness of public institutions, which they see as broken and in dire need of repair.

Trust is at the heart of the problem, and reconstructing people's faith in government is getting the attention of the nation's top leaders. President Clinton has been "pitching trust to skeptics" or Americans who lack confidence in their government. According to the president, "The central tenet of every democracy in the end is trust" (Ifill, 1993, p. A10). Vice President Al Gore, leading the latest charge to reinvent government, says ineffective administrative systems are not the fault of people who work in them. The heart of the problem is embedded in the job roles, workplace rules, and conditions "that still convey the message that workers aren't trusted" (Gore, 1993, p. 68). Low trust is the truth being discovered yet again as the cause and consequence of organizational arrangements and management practices that strangle individual achievement and institutional accomplishment.

The prescription for repairing public administration is simple:

"You've got to trust. People don't come to work with the intent of screwing it up every day. They come here to make it better" (Goins, 1993, p. 69). The enduring problem is that employees in the public service are not trusted, and therefore not enabled, to make government perform better.

Trust is faith in people, their motivations, and their capacities. Trust in people at work reflects the faith that workers can face the reality of a work situation and *will* work to do something about it. No organization can realize high performance without the energy and social cohesion supplied by trust.

Trust is not inevitable. It is nurtured or destroyed by assumptions that people who run organizations hold about subordinates. Trust or distrust is embedded in the work processes and governance systems institutionalized in response to those assumptions. Trust is the outcome of *choices* that leaders make on how organizational affairs will be handled.

In public organizations the root problem is reliance on excessively bureaucratic organizational arrangements, designed for operating environments that no longer exist. These outmoded structures and their equally out-of-date low-trust operating philosophies trap and suffocate people. They intimidate, promote fear, and discourage innovation. They encourage defensive behavior and interfere with learning. They systematically undermine trust and subvert achievement.

This book is about trust, how it functions, and why it is so consequential in the workplace. Its message can be summed up in three connections, all leading to high performance.

1. *Trust is essential.* There is no organization without trust. Trust is what holds the social fabric of organizations together. Trust is an essential aspect of community. No social system or community can operate effectively without some measure of mutual faith among members. Fear cannot substitute for trust. It cannot bond people in ways that make things happen with the same kind of ease that trust can. Authoritarianism cannot substitute for trust. It can

influence only what it can control and there are limits to control in organizations.

2. *Trust is truth.* Trust enables employees and managers to face up to the truth of their working situation. Organizations make choices about how they will structure and manage work processes, and those choices influence levels of trust and the extent that employees have control over their work. Organizations that rely on low-trust bureaucratic work arrangements distort the truth of the working situation and suppress the productive potential of employees. Organizations that employ more trust-based methods are reality centered and perform better. There is little truth in organizations without trust. In low-trust organizations, more is hidden than is revealed.

3. *Trust is survival.* Facing up to the truth through trust enables people to reduce defensive behaviors and open themselves up to learning. In the contemporary world of work, organizations that are unable to exploit the experience, knowhow, information, and intelligence of people down the line are doomed to fail. Organizations are learning systems and need to be managed in a fashion that liberates, rather than restrains, people's knowledge.

In these pages, I demonstrate how key organizational processes can be managed in ways that build trust. The underlying theme is that high-trust work organizations liberate employees' full potential, give them greater control over their jobs, and promote independence, participation, open communications, organizational justice, critical learning, and more democratic forms of governance. The trust connections in organizations are extensive. Managing trust requires dealing with all aspects of organizational behavior.

It is essential to understand, if we are to come to grips with how trust works, that people react directly and in kind to the amount of trust directed at them. Because of the choices that organizations make about how much they are willing to trust or empower their employees, they reap what they sow in terms of individual commitment, involvement, identification, loyalty, motivation, and achievement.

Why Trust Matters

Trust holds organizations together. It has been described as an integrative mechanism that creates and sustains solidarity in social systems (Barber, 1983; Blau, 1964). Nothing happens without trust. It provides the lubrication that makes it possible for organizations to work (Bennis and Nanus, 1985). Trust is associated with productivity (Golembiewski and McConkie, 1975; Rotter, 1967), group performance (Zand, 1972; Boss, 1978), cooperation and conflict (Deutsch, 1973; Loomis, 1959; Sherif, 1966), leadership styles (Likert, 1967), managerial assumptions about workers (McGregor, 1960), need satisfaction (Maslow, 1954), organizational change and development (Golembiewski, 1986), participation (Miles and Ritchie, 1984), communication (Mellinger, 1956), stress and burnout (Golembiewski, Munzenrider, and Stevenson, 1986), "psychological contracts" or the unwritten mutual expectations between individuals and their employers (Argyris, 1960), and the quality of labor-management relations (Reich, 1987).

These do not exhaust the full range of attachments. Levels of trust are a measure of system power in high-performing organizations. While the subject of trust receives considerable notice, there is very little real grasp of how it is created and sustained. Despite widespread agreement that it is crucial for organizational effectiveness, there is but a piecemeal understanding of why this is so. The answer lies in the psychological reactions that trust engenders in individuals and how these reactions influence learning and behavior in organizations. The next chapter explores this.

The Contemporary Crisis of Trust

Trust is much lower in most groups and organizations than is desirable and necessary (French and Bell, 1984). Where does the crisis exist exactly? The evidence is that it is everywhere. In society at large, fully 43 percent of Americans are reported to be cynics who see "selfishness and fakery at the core of human nature" (Kanter and Mirvis, 1989, pp. 1, 2). These same people act in accordance with these negative beliefs. At work they are less open to new experiences or the influence of other people. They are always wary of being manipulated or disappointed. In the long run, this suspicious stance is a drag on organizational performance and adds costs.

Confidence in public institutions has been in a steady decline in recent years (Lipset and Schneider, 1987). An October 1992 Time/CNN poll showed that 63 percent of respondents had little or no faith that government leaders "talk straight" and fully 75 percent reported that there was less honesty in government than there had been ten years ago (Gray, 1992, p. 32). Prior to the Vietnam War, eight out of ten people said they trusted people in Washington to do what was right most of the time. In 1994, less than one third of the people felt that way (Broder, 1994). These attitudes extend to the workplace.

Many Americans go to their jobs with guarded, suspicious attitudes, with little confidence in the motives of organizational agents and little faith that they will not be exploited or taken advantage of. Fear and distrust are all too prevalent in the contemporary workplace. The behaviors fostered by such feelings are corrosive and debilitating to those who harbor them and to their organizations.

In the new world of work, the trust gap is widening. *Fortune* reported that "people below the acme of the corporate pyramid trust those on top just about as far as they can throw a Gulfstream IV, with shower" (Farnham, 1989, p.56). In the private sector, the 1980s saw the end of the psychological contract that promised ever increasing salaries and guaranteed career mobility in return for faithful service. People's trust in their organizations has been stretched to the breaking point (Kanter, 1989). Nearly one million managers and their immediate staff lost their jobs in the private sector as downsizing became a way of life. Now similar trends are emerging in the public sector.

Already there are reports that reductions in force (RIFs) are likely in the new reinventing-government schemes, despite promises that staff layoff could be avoided by either attrition (current rates are at historic lows in the federal government) or buyouts (Congress got to them so late that mainly top officials will benefit during the first round). In fact, if past is prologue, Congress is likely to grasp all the immediate cost-savings ideas it can and ignore all the other proposals that require investing in deeper, long-term change strategies.

White-collar jobless became the new majority when their unemployment exceeded blue-collar joblessness in early 1993 by 200,000 workers, the first such gap on record (Roach, 1993). And the situation is not getting better. Wearing a necktie, once an indicator of security as well as success, no longer carries the same meaning. Among blue-collar workers, layoffs were always part of the bargain. Many planned for the predictable RIFs and counted on the equally anticipated callbacks. But the recent decade has been different. No one is safe and, when a layoff occurs, it is very possible that no one will be recalled.

The biggest casualty found among all workers who suffered through the long recession at the beginning of the 1990s and the jobless recovery is that the mutual loyalty between employees and employers is being replaced by mistrust, and not just because job security is threatened by the vagaries of the business cycle or attempts to reduce the size of government. Managers report that there is a lack of honest, open communication and a failure to treat employees with respect and dignity. Employees are misled about future closings, while at the same time top executives allow the gap between their rewards and those of other employees to escalate beyond reasonable proportions (Horton and Reid, 1991). In fact, some executives at top companies are seeing their salaries raised *because* they forced mass layoffs in their organizations. While some workers are thrown from organizations with meager benefits, their leaders drift safely to earth wearing golden parachutes. The real harm done by such selfishness undermines organizations because it subverts shared commitment and spawns cynicism and indifference among employees (Samuelson, 1991).

It is increasingly understood that organizations—whether public or private—can no longer guarantee the protection they once did. This is not entirely because they are uncaring or mean-spirited. Competitiveness, efficiency breakthroughs, changes in technology, and shrinking resources are more and more the norm in both the private and public sectors. They make job security assurances impossible.

If an organization cannot ensure job protection, however, it does not mean that building trust is impossible. Employers can still enable people to learn and develop marketable skills. Staff members can have confidence that their work lives will be developmental and fulfilling even within the stern operating constraints of modern institutions. More than anything else, that means they will have a chance to develop their capabilities and get to show what they know how to do. This increases their employability, which is the new deal at work (Kanter, 1989).

The public case is still better with respect to job security. The belief that a public job is relatively more secure still holds, but it is less reliable than it used to be. I spend time every year teaching at military bases in the Pacific. Over the last couple of years, I have witnessed the stress on highly capable personnel increase as they watch their careers go up in smoke. There was a time when, if they performed well and made a commitment to the armed services, they could reasonably expect a good chance to serve for twenty years or maybe more. But that is no longer the case. The world has changed and they too face drawdowns and retrenchment in a profession that was once recession-proof. The same is true for postal workers, federal civilian employees, university professors, and a host of others. Every day comes new announcements about downsizing in government.

A recent survey of federal employees demonstrated that only 44 percent of respondents indicated that they trusted their agencies (Rivenbark, 1992). In yet another analysis, a significant number of employees also expressed a lack of confidence in their first-level supervisors (U.S. Merit Systems Protection Board, 1992). Since supervisors are the people responsible for a good deal of hiring, firing, promoting, evaluating, rewarding, punishing, and negotiating work roles, these data are very disturbing. A recent survey of more than 700,000 U.S. Postal Service employees showed that only 37 percent believed the information they received from the service, only 41 percent found the service to be good or very good in terms of trustworthiness, and a scant 16 percent had faith that anything would be done about problems identified in the survey ("Survey of Employees . . .," 1993).

The Problem Outside

The external environment of public organizations is hardly conducive to building trust. The public sector has been buffeted by resource scarcity for more than a decade. It has suffered from an intensification of the business-is-better mentality, and the ability to meet a payroll persists as a superior claim to legitimacy in managing public enterprises. Calls for choice and contracting of government services abound and, lately, a stampede of enthusiasm for reinventing, revitalizing, reengineering, and rethinking government is evident.

These latest innovations hold some promise for improving citizen faith in public institutions, *if* they do not lead to the kind of fiscal freewheeling and lack of accountability that invites even more suspicion and misanthropic bureaucrat bashing (Goodsell, 1993). Some of the stories trotted out to justify the reinventing-government theme, unfortunately, do smack of bureaucrat bashing. Many seem excessively severe. At the very least, they run the line on reinforcing the worst prejudices that people have about government.

For example, how many government workers does it take to change a lightbulb? Forty-three, according to a safety procedure proposed at a federal nuclear weapons plant. The idea would have added a significant number of worker hours to the present system.

What did not get a lot of play was that the lightbulb warns workers of nuclear accidents. A nuclear plant is not a local mini-mart. The consequences for system failure are huge. Maybe a thirty-three–step plan to deal with a warning light is appropriate. Using this story to justify reinvention is certainly dramatic, but it overly simplifies the issue of what a lightbulb represents in some public agencies. It also makes a joke out of the issue of public safety. After the Three Mile Island incident, no one would have cared much if it took a hundred steps to get a disaster warning light working correctly.

Another example: One of the usual suspects rounded up by the reinvention folks is the federal personnel system. There is no doubt that it is badly in need of reform. An entire chapter of this book is devoted to the low-trust premises that underwrite federal personnel policy. However, the idea that the federal personnel manual is 10,000 pages and weighs in at over 1,000 pounds trivializes the problems of human resources administration in the federal sector and appeals to the worst instincts of antigovernment zealots. The collection of what appears as an excessive amount of rules is in direct response to real experiences with the fraud, corruption, and abuse that attended the spoils system, dishonest privatization schemes, the systematic destruction of whistleblowers, and ever-present political pressures for favoritism in appointments and promotions.

Public employees continue to be the victims of attacks "from the malicious to the naive [that] demean the value of public service" and erode confidence (Holzer and Rabin, 1987, p. 4). They inspire the kind of "humor" that *Time* magazine used to introduce the reinventing-government enterprise, in a story entitled "Gorezilla Zaps the System": "The biggest lie in America, other than 'The check is in the mail,' is 'I'm from the government, and I'm here to help you.' The Pentagon calls its new weapon the Civil Servant. Reason: it won't work and can't be fired. Did you hear the one about the clerk who needed a full week to fill out all the papers to comply with the requirements of the government's latest initiative, the Paperwork Reduction Act?" (Church, 1993, p. 25).

This is bureaucrat bashing plain and simple. It continues the erosion of public confidence in government. It also lets politicians and the citizenry off the hook when it comes to accepting well-deserved responsibility for the state of government in America today.

Is it worth the effort to try to improve intraorganizational trust if the operating environment of public institutions is so hostile? What is the point, after all? Is it not hopeless? The answer is *no!* Perhaps it is better to ask, what is the alternative?

Faith in public institutions will be restored when they perform better. Confidence in government will improve when it is able to get the credit it deserves for producing quality work. Environments cannot be controlled. What can be managed better is how we run our organizations. That is where we must begin. Anything less is abandoning the field to those who hate government, who find joy in running it down, and who prosper from a culture of political cynicism. Restoring trust begins with strengthening the organizations that citizens experience in their lives and having faith that ultimately high-performing public organizations, founded upon trust, will accumulate the positive support they will have earned.

A thoughtful, and generally positive, approach to introducing the need for reforming government, and one that also confronts directly the issue of whether or not the trial of improving trust government is worth the effort, is embodied in the recently released work by the National Commission on the State and Local Public Service. Frank J. Thompson, in the introduction to a book-length treatment of the commission's work (Thompson, 1993), notes that the United States has a very distinctive political culture built on mistrust. This institutionalized mistrust constantly erodes public confidence and undermines efforts to revitalize the public service at every level. However, Thompson is an optimist. He offers three reasons for trying to revitalize, reinvigorate, and rebuild the public service:

1. Public organizations can be made to perform better.

2. More effective public agencies would be more "democratically responsive and accountable" (p.2).

3. Finally, citizens would see a revitalized government more favorably if they had better experience with it.

No one considers any of this easy. However, overcoming mistrust is not impossible despite the tenacious obstacles that stand in the way. It is difficult to introduce new technologies and a more democratic workplace in the face of bureaucratic obstacles, but it is not impossible.

The Problem Inside

The bureaucratic model of organizations dominates the public landscape. It has its virtues and remains the most common form in modern society. Its underlying organizing assumptions are, however, decidedly low trust.

In bureaucracy, hierarchy is the central devising principle, work roles are narrowly defined, a premium is placed on impersonality in relationships, control is maximized, efficiency is prized, secrecy is a virtue, and means rather than ends receive the lion's share of attention.

Bureaucracy is explicitly unfriendly to the idea of trust. It attempts to make trust irrelevant by specifying in advance every behavior, each obligation, and the norms that guide encounters between individuals. The functionary and the professional who impersonally represent bureaucracy are guided by external standards that deny the internal norms upon which trusting social relations must rely. Every aspect of bureaucratic work denies the significance of creating social capital among members. It is narrowminded, closed to criticism, form-oriented. In the end, it is the rules that must be trusted, the procedures that confidence is placed in, and the legal authority of the superior institution that one's faith is placed in. Bureaucracy is a monument to institutionalized mistrust and emotional control.

The Sticking Power of Bureaucracy

Despite evidence that alternative patterns of work organizations, underwritten by high-trust premises, are both possible and necessary, the bureaucratic model has yielded grudgingly, if at all, to fresh designs.

There are several reasons why so few organizations have successfully made the transition from bureaucratic to high-performing work systems. One is that there is a certain inertia in organizations that defies any type of change.

A second is that change requires more resources. What we may call the "investment paradox" is that moving from bureaucratic to high-performing work systems demands the investment of considerable resources in, for instance, staff training and development and new technology. It is evident that society is not prepared to make these contributions. Even if public leadership was ready to adopt a high-investment strategy, it simply does not have the means to do so.

A third problem in diffusing high performance is organizational leadership that is not prepared to share power, authority, and responsibility with employees throughout the organization. Giving effective voice to subordinates is uncharted territory for many organizational leaders, and many are clearly threatened by it. This is rational behavior, given the number of supervisorial and managerial jobs lost during the current downsizing and retrenchment period in both public and private organizations. Put simply, there is a clear collision between changing bureaucratic organizations and established authority and power relations.

A fourth problem is that of technology. Management in every sector of the economy appears ambivalent about how to treat technology. Technology can serve the bureaucratic regime by perpetuating or even intensifying the standardization, surveillance, specialization, and fragmentation of work processes, or it can restructure work to promote flexible team processes and free up the knowhow of line staff. Because the impetus for transforming organizations is driven more and more by immediate financial or political crises, using technology to extend the logic of mass production systems seems the easy way out. This is because it fits the prevailing management ideology, established organizational structure, job design, and human resource practices.

A fifth problem is unions. The public sector is heavily unionized, but changes in management philosophy rarely are explicit about the role of unions in transforming work organizations. One could easily argue that the sort of participative management and empowerment designs of transformation programs are nicely accommodated by the collective bargaining process. Collective bargaining gets precious little attention in discussions of how to create high-performing work organizations even though the topics ordinarily addressed within the scope of negotiation have a lot to do with how well organizations perform.

Tellingly, many of the innovations that preceded the latest attempts at transforming organizations were designed in large part as union-avoidance strategies. Unions are almost not mentioned at all, for instance, in the Baldrige criteria used to award business organizations that have achieved quality by empowering their employees through various participation and involvement schemes. The omission is significant. Unions can help high performance become a reality or they can be a drag on achievement. Organizational leaders have a choice about the kind of labor relations they will have. It is a mistake to believe that public organizations can be reformed without the involvement of unions and without any regard for the collective bargaining process.

A sixth reason transforming organizations is so difficult is that organizations fail to integrate their human resource and industrial relations policies to support substantial strategic changes such as building trust. Organizations are used to disaggregating problems into small pieces and have difficulty thinking holistically about how to put themselves back together again to gain system power. Trust is part of the social fabric of work institutions and cannot be piecemealed into existence.

Seventh, people in a position to change public organizations work with very short time horizons. They are not around very long in comparison to their private-sector counterparts, and reforming systems is a major and politically thankless undertaking in most instances. Shorter-term goals with bigger, more immediate political payoffs get their attention. The problem of institutionalizing long-term change in public bureaucracy, given the rapid turnover of top executives and the often miserable transition of their replacements, is a major impediment to sustaining change programs.

Eighth, a lot of what passes for management and organization reform has a short shelf life. This is partly because of the insidious combination of all the forces already cited, which conspire to subvert real change. In the past few years, would-be reformers have witnessed the Civil Service Reform Act of 1978, the Grace Commission, Volcker Commission, Winter Commission, Total Quality Management, Japanese management, the Excellence Movement, and now a bunch of "re-" words like reinventing, rediscovering, and revitalizing government. All the plans seem to suffer the same fate. Each new method is greeted with a fair measure of enthusiasm from zealots before falling out of favor. Each is then replaced by yet another heralded scheme before the cycle repeats itself. Few of the promising ideas are ever fully implemented and none survives long enough to have its effects evaluated. The problem seems to lie more with the reformers than the reforms.

Ninth, government innovations in controversial public policy areas are likely to offend powerful political interests. Government reform only superficially builds political capital. It can also be a headache for some organized interests, particularly those who like the status quo. Political leaders are often suspicious of government managers and are not eager to grant them autonomy, decentralization, and more control.

The Challenge to Leaders

Organizational leaders in the public sector, then, are severely tested in three ways when it comes to inducing trust. First, public organizations, and those who lead them, are not trusted by the general population. Confidence in most of America's institutions is steadily eroding, and opinions about government are especially harsh. Second, these attitudes combine with the low-trust effects of bureaucratic norms, which are pervasive in the public sector. Third, a host of promising innovations designed, in part, to restore public and employee trust face several barriers that prevent them from being institutionalized except in a few organizations.

It is not a very encouraging picture. However, it is not hopeless. Study after study shows that the public wants to trust government and employees yearn to trust their organizations. The public wants better services from public agencies. The fact is that the constituencies for change exist, as does the technology to make it happen. Before detailing what might be done, however, it is important to understand what trust is and how it works.

2

Organizational Performance and the Dynamics of Trust

Despite its wide usage, definitions of the word *trust* are rare. According to Bennis and Nanus (1985), trust, like leadership, is elusive and difficult to comprehend. Barber (1983) supports the view that trust and related ideas, like faith and confidence, are not well defined and represent a "conceptual morass."

However, a review of various studies pertaining to trust does suggest some threads that intertwine into a common weave. The key elements involve assumptions about people's motives, predictability, integrity, honesty, moral character, and credibility in situations where a measure of dependency is present. In the workplace, management makes judgments about workers with respect to these six issues and establishes a system of governance that reflects its beliefs. The key to understanding trust is that it is a reciprocal attitude, which simply means that people usually get back what they give. In organizational terms, the judgments that an organization makes about the character of its workforce are often self-fulfilling.

Trust involves the process of drawing an inference about the motive of a person, group, or institution for acting in a certain way.

People use past behavior or reputation to measure whether to trust someone (Dasgupta, 1988). On an individual basis, to the extent we do not trust someone, we will feel the need to keep a careful watch over that person and to protect ourselves (Strickland, 1958).

Trust also has to do with predictability, which means we can foretell a person's behavior. To inspire trust, the conduct of the other person can be positive or negative as long as it is reliable. We can trust a person to be reliably untrustworthy as well as trustworthy. In both cases, we know what to expect—good and bad—and can act accordingly. People do, obviously, prefer trustworthy behavior. The implication for managerial practice is to be trustworthy and consistent.

Since trust involves dependency, it raises the issue of harm. Trust involves *risk* that our willingness to invest our faith will leave us worse off in a situation where our recourse is limited, if it exists at all. The implication for work behavior is straightforward. People will not try something innovative, or depart from the customary way of doing things, if they feel that taking a risk invites punishment. People need to feel safe to change and to try something new.

In brief, trust can be summarized as faith or confidence in the intentions and actions of a person or group to be ethical, fair, and nonthreatening concerning the rights and interests of others in social exchange relationships (Carnevale, 1988). It also relates to a willingness to place ourselves in jeopardy, to become vulnerable, that is, to take the chance that our dependency will not be exploited (Eddy, 1981). It means giving another party the benefit of the doubt in a situation that we cannot fully control. Mistrust, on the other hand, suggests a belief that someone's intentions and motives are not always what they appear; that a person is insincere, unethical, has ulterior motives, or is unwilling to honor an agreement. Such a person is regarded as threatening in organizational settings (Mellinger, 1956).

These characteristics may be generalized from the individual to the group and, ultimately, to the organization itself. But regardless of the level of analysis, the consequence of mistrust is always the same: People who perceive the environment as untrustworthy will act defensively to protect themselves from harm.

Dynamics of Institutionalized Trust

Trust permeates every aspect of associations; it is a mistake to see it as grounded in interpersonal dynamics alone. In addition to the dynamics of human relations subsystems, expressions of trust can also be uncovered in the structural, political, and symbolic dimensions of organizational life. Structural considerations involve how organizations and job roles are constructed. Political factors entail power relations, competition, and negotiations. Symbolic catalysts consist of the meanings or interpretations people give to their experiences.

Trust is *institutionalized* in an organization's rules, roles, and relations (Fox, 1974a). That means it is embedded in everything an organization does or tries to do. It is explicit and implicit. It is in the climate and culture. It is found in every interpersonal encounter, at every meeting. It is displayed in how outsiders are treated. It permeates organizations.

Trust is explicit in how an organization is arranged (the configuration of its hierarchical levels and specialized units), expressed in the variability of job and work process design, evident in the personnel system's incentive patterns, and apparent in how people are treated by supervisors. It also manifests itself in physical work arrangements. These elements can add up to high-trust or low-trust work cultures.

An example of a low-trust work culture is the U.S. Postal Service. As is well known, there have been a series of tragic shootings in recent years. One investigative television show looked for causes of the violence. Reporters found a generally bureaucratic and terribly stressful work environment, where employees performed impoverished, mind-numbing jobs and where supervisors were constantly overlooking their activities. Many of the supervisors were young and not very experienced in moving the mail. They moved around the workfloor with calculators in their hands to monitor production, or watched workers from observation slits built above the workfloor. Machines counted errors, and employees could expect to see a supervisor if too many were made. Job security was low as the postal service, facing competitive pressures, began downsizing its workforce. The reduction was supposed to come as a result of attrition but employees felt that management was using every infraction of the rules, no matter how trivial, to justify terminating workers in order to get the workforce scaled down at an even faster rate. What was created was a low-trust, bureaucratic mail factory where mistrust prevailed. In extreme cases, the climate edged toward violence. All the workers interviewed said they were not surprised when the shootings came.

For an organization, how it chooses to organize and operate symbolizes its assumptions about how much it trusts its members. An organization makes choices about whether communication systems are open or closed, decides whether jobs allow some measure of autonomy or are carefully regulated, shows confidence in the knowhow of its members by encouraging participation in decision making or devalues the intelligence of staff by ignoring their advice. It reaches for moral involvement and mutual commitment or relies excessively on transactional or contractual means to enforce agreements. It encourages or suppresses voice and demonstrates a tolerance or resistance of dissent. It drives at ensuring procedural justice or is arbitrary in disciplining members. It earns a reputation for ethical conduct in dealings with employees and clients or is greeted with well-deserved cynicism by both. It favors either explicit formalisms or implicit values.

Trust or mistrust are not destiny. These feelings originate from the confluence of *choices* organizations make about how they will be designed and managed. Significantly, when it comes to trust, organizations are always on trial.

The patterns organizations choose to govern themselves mean something to employees, and they choose to commit themselves accordingly. They elect to collaborate, cooperate, and invest themselves in those situations which they interpret as valuing them and their interests. Or they become alienated, withdrawn, or even hostile in response to the injustice of violated trust (Zand, 1972).

For an individual, trust is a distinct work-related attitude and derives, in part, from a person's psychological predispositions and beliefs. People come to work with a propensity involving trust based on their perceptions and life experiences. They may be guarded, suspicious, and careful about what they say and do, or they may be open and authentic. But despite individual tendencies, the most powerful determinants of trust at work are within the control of the organization.

Reciprocal Trust

By how organizations choose to function, they reinforce people's inclination to trust. The combination of influences manifest in various organizational subsystems reinforces initial wariness or justifies original expressions of confidence. This is because trust is a reciprocal attitude: people comprehend and reflect the trust aimed at them.

The give-and-take aspect of trust works this way: When we see others acting in ways that imply that they trust us, we become more disposed to reciprocate by trusting in them more. Conversely, we come to distrust those whose actions appear to violate our trust or to show that they distrust us (Lewis and Weigert, 1985).

Luhmann (1979, p. 73) characterizes this idea of returning, in kind, whatever trust has been given, as "reciprocal escalation": "Someone who sees himself as the object of . . . expressions of distrust will hardly be disposed to look at himself from the perspective of distrust and seek the cause of it in himself . . . he will respond with distrust himself."

Trust, then, has a circular, self-heightening quality; expressions of trust beget trust and distrust engenders distrust. Trust and distrust feed on themselves. Once a cycle is created, it tends to intensify and

FIGURE 2.1. The Dynamics of Trust and Organizational Learning.

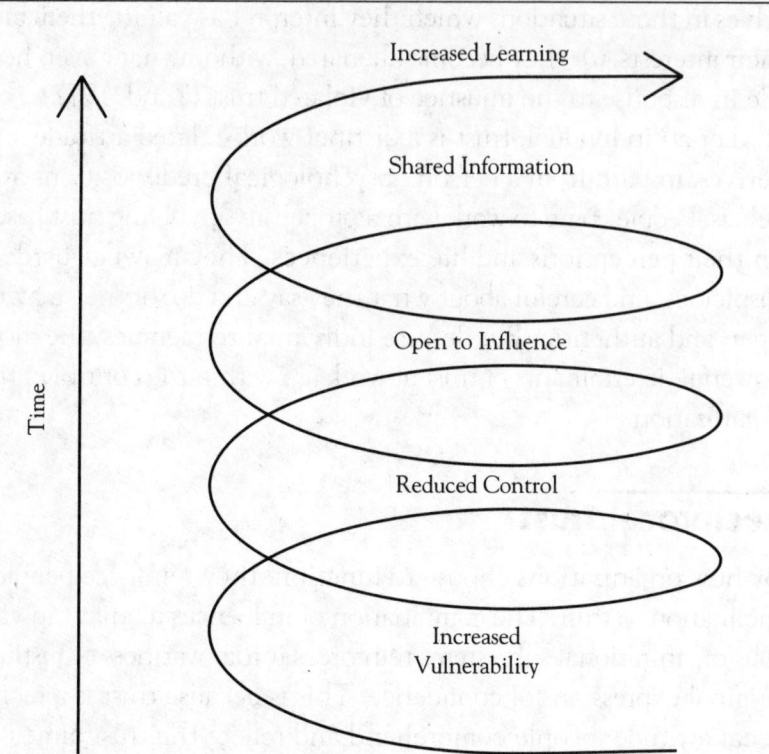

Adapted from Zand (1972) and Golembiewski and McConkie (1975).

fortify itself (Golembiewski and McConkie, 1975; Zand, 1972). This self-reinforcing dynamic is the key to grasping how interpersonal and situational factors interact to trigger and sustain trust or distrust in organizations. Moreover, it is central to understanding how trust influences learning (see Figure 2.1).

When people trust another person, they allow themselves to become more vulnerable. They are willing to take risks in a situation where the behavior of that other person may do them harm. At the same time, they give up some of their self-protective need to control the situation. They are more willing to accept interdependence with others, and need fewer rules or constraints to control other people's behavior. They have greater confidence that others will do what they agree to. The increase in vulnerability through trust, combined with the lessening of the need for control, opens people to the influence of others. They are able to accept influence in the selection of goals, choice of methods, and evaluation of progress.

These dynamics enable the disclosure of necessary communication and information. People who are not preoccupied with self-protection are free to disclose more relevant, accurate, and complete data about the problem and about their thoughts and feelings. Then they are able to learn. In other words, they are capable of modifying how they perceive events or adjusting their behavior because of new information or experiences. As individuals and groups do this, the foundation of organizational learning is initially established.

The physics of trust are degenerative or regenerative. Degenerative low-trust forces lead to a depressed sense of personal efficacy, defensiveness, and a don't-rock-the-boat mentality. Regenerative or high-trust processes, on the other hand, encourage risk taking, openness, and confidence in facing and solving problems (Golembiewski, 1985). Trust, in these cases, means "I don't have to defend," "I can live without fear," "I can do my best, take a risk, try something new, and, if it doesn't work, it will be all right."

Fear, Defensive Behavior, and Learning

Gibb (1978, pp. 31–32) details the consequences of fear for trust in social relationships: "When fears are high, relative to trust level, I tend to try to control my reactions and yours. My energies are directed toward discovering and creating boundaries, legalities, rules, contracts, protective devices, and various structures that will embody the controls that seem necessary to keep life in order. . . . Fear predisposes a person to overperceive and overreact to the significance of authority and power figures, and the importance of management and control."

Fear creates a significant barrier to trust, quality, productivity,

FIGURE 2.2. The Cycle of Mistrust, Defensive Conduct, and Learning Impairment.

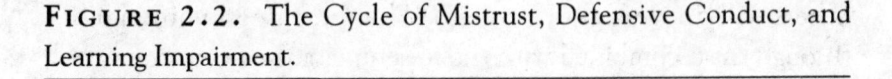

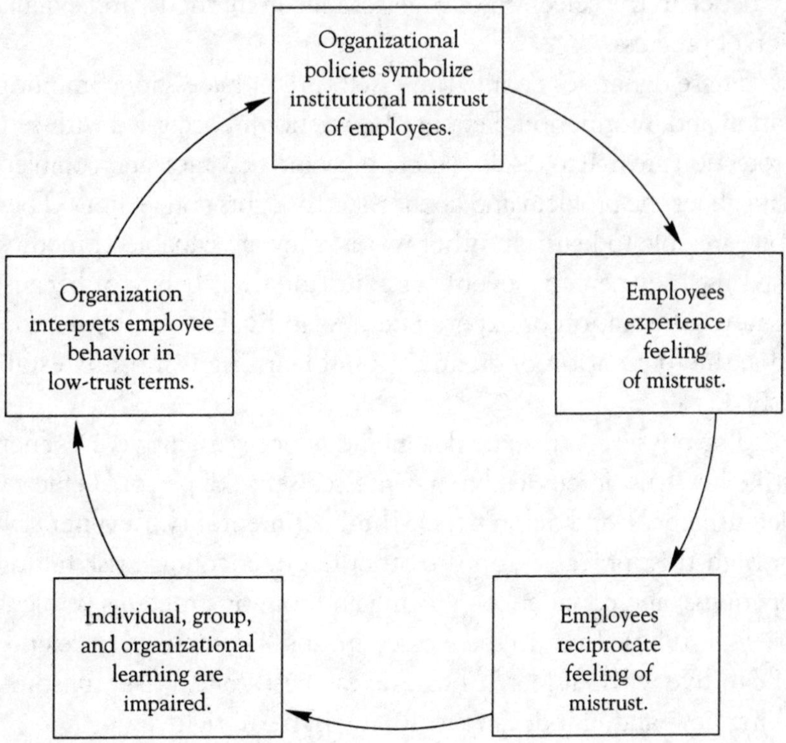

and innovation (Deming, 1986; Ryan and Oestreich, 1993; Kanter and Mirvis, 1989). These connections alone are reason enough for enlarging trust and security on the job. However, the most important rationale for augmenting trust and reducing apprehension is that the defensive routines of fearful people interfere with their ability to learn. This is the central theme of this book.

Latent fear destroys learning. As Gibb (1961, p. 144) emphasizes, fearful, low-trust people are too preoccupied to learn effectively when they have to concentrate on "how [they] appear to others, how [they] may be seen more favorably, how [they] may win, dominate, impress, or escape punishment, and, or, how [they] may avoid or mitigate a perceived or anticipated attack." Stated differ-ently, to protect themselves from the social uncertainty that is added to the objective uncertainty that exists in any situation (Zand, 1972), fearful, low-trust people engage in distancing, cam-ouflaging, mask maintenance, and role-barricading behaviors.

The degenerative relationship between mistrust, defensive con-duct, and the impairment of organizational learning is cyclical in nature (see Figure 2.2).

Work policies in organizations symbolize how much employees are trusted. In low-trust situations, employees experience narrowly specialized jobs that do not allow for much participation or involvement on their part. Motivation is manipulated rather than inspired; fear pervades the workplace. Leadership is controlling.

As the next step in the cycle, employees experience the mis-trust directed toward them. Their sense of self-efficacy is dimin-ished, and they feel little ability to improve their situation or to influence others. They recognize the pressure to conform and per-ceive the work environment as threatening. They are made to feel insecure.

In turn, employees reciprocate mistrust by increasing their defensive posture. They protect themselves by being careful in their interaction with others. They are unwilling to disclose accurate data to others, and so the flow of communication is reduced. Employees are more concerned with dependable role behavior than high com-mitment to the organization.

The result of these dynamics is that individual, group, and orga-nizational learning are impaired because employees are less able to process critical feedback from their work experiences. They are closed off from such experiences. They avoid critical thinking and the spirit of inquiry so necessary for new learning. Effective collab-oration with others is destroyed.

As the final step in the cycle, organizations see that employees demonstrate little capacity for self-management, and—the final part of the cycle—interpret that behavior as low capability and low commitment. Their response is to intensify control, and so the low-

trust cycle is repeated. Unless institutionalized management practices change and become symbolic of greater confidence in staff, the
cycle will continue indefinitely.

It is this interference with learning that defeats high performance among individuals, groups, and organizations. The connections are clear. As Senge (1990, p. 139) aptly puts it, "Organizations
learn only through individuals who learn. Individual learning does
not guarantee organizational learning. But without it no organizational learning occurs."

High-Performance Learning Systems

There is wide agreement that modern organizations should be
appreciated as open systems where feedback from the environment
facilitates better performance. "Feedback" is just another name for
learning. Learning relies on the ability to gain enhanced knowledge
and understanding from experience and use them to improve
awareness and actions. Learning means more than developing the
capacity to simply adapt and survive. It also means the ability to
process and build upon new knowledge to innovate and create
(Senge, 1990).

Organizations are learning systems. Some are better than others. In organizations that learn poorly, the cause can be traced to
the way they are designed and managed, and the way individuals
have been taught to think and interact (Senge, 1990). In these
instances, learning disabilities are embedded, in part, in managers'
deeply internalized theories about the nature of people and whether
they can be trusted. The problem in contemporary organizations is
that the dominant underlying management philosophy is of the
low-trust variety, more suitable (if it ever was correct) for the
smokestack and assembly-line age that flourished at the beginning
of the century.

The majority of America's modern workplaces, both public and
private, were modeled after the manufacturing model pioneered
during the early 1900s and have not changed. Indeed, a recent

study investigating why America's productivity growth has slowed to a crawl in recent years found that fully 95 percent of American organizations cling to the traditional turn-of-the-century form of work design and its dreary characteristics (National Center on Education and the Economy, 1990). The typical American workplace is still a place where a majority of employees are still expected to check their brains at the door (Committee on the Evolution of Work, 1994).

Admittedly, the mass production, bureaucratic model was not without value. It fit the demands of America's early period of industrialization and was able to provide high volumes of standardized goods at affordable prices. It resulted in Americans enjoying the highest standard of living in the world. Close supervision, highly specialized jobs, the values of efficiency and economy, and predictability through control paid off. In the public sector, the objective was similar. The goal was to provide greater access to mass-produced services like basic education, sanitation, transportation, law enforcement, and fire protection (Carnevale, 1992).

Now things have changed. Organizations face new performance standards that require a fresh set of assumptions about people and their capabilities. These new performance standards include not just efficiency and economy but also quality, variety, customization, convenience, and timeliness (Carnevale, 1991). These criteria represent a broader notion of effectiveness and productivity and demand greater competencies and involvement from all workers, especially front-line personnel.

New performance standards compel broader and deeper skills. The emerging workplace is properly conceptualized as a learning environment where high performance depends on fully utilizing the abilities of everyone. What is required is both lower-level or single-loop learning, which means knowing how to repeat past behaviors and detecting and correcting errors within a given set of rules, and higher-level or double-loop learning, which involves the faculty to discern when central norms, frames of reference, and basic assumptions need to be changed (Argyris and Shon, 1978; Fiol and Lyles,

1985). At its heart, the difference between ordinary performance and high performance is the distinction between single- and double-loop learning. At issue is how to liberate the power that higher-order learning represents. Successful organizations demonstrate an ability to learn from the bottom up and at every level. The key is to increase employees' scope of action, giving them the capacity not just to execute actions determined elsewhere but to conceive them in the first place.

At the heart of the shift in expectations concerning organizational performance is a new cognitive paradigm that encourages learning created by a management philosophy based on trust. More than that, it is an intellectual archetype that actually legitimizes and employs learning no matter where it occurs in the organization. In that sense, it is truly revolutionary.

Learning organizations can be distinguished from traditional controlling organizations and the wariness they engender among people. The key difference is that deeply ingrained defensiveness so characteristic of low-trust, traditional bureaucratic organizations undermines necessary learning. Trust expedites learning. Healthy learning organizations are managed with the objective of liberating and using employee knowhow to improve work processes. The emancipation of employee knowhow is enabled through a different philosophy of organization and job design, communication patterns, labor-management relations, participatory methods, and other processes that reduce the climate of fear and allow staff the necessary psychological peace of mind to fully engage their work.

A fresh trust-centered approach to management is demanded in the evolving world of work. The postmodern system of administration is less bureaucratic, authoritarian, and control-oriented. These behaviors gain only obedience and lower-order involvement. They discourage innovation and creativity. The alternative high-trust strategy is based on a different set of skills and competencies. These encourage coaching, facilitating, and teaching. They aim to strengthen the knowledge base of the organization and then let employees have some operating room to attack problems. In the high-trust learning model, trust is a weapon to help organizations adapt, compete, and survive. It is the tool that releases employee knowhow.

In summary, the dynamics of trust suggest several things. First, trust is a momentous factor in organizational life, and there is persistent evidence of a widening trust gap in the workplace, particularly in public organizations. Second, people's individual predispositions to trust or mistrust are reinforced by monitoring and attributing meaning to organizational processes and events. Third, employees reciprocate the kind of trust directed toward them. Fourth, levels of trust determine the amount of defensive behavior in organizations, which, in turn, conditions the capacity for individual, group, and system learning.

3

Overcoming Barriers to Trust

If higher levels of trust are to be constructed, organizations must recognize assumptions they hold about the motivations and capabilities of people at work because these assumptions drive their management methods. Beliefs about human nature have shaped the response to the perennial problem of organizations: how to motivate the commitment of individuals and groups to achieve organizational goals.

Since people first organized to accomplish some goal, there has been a struggle to discover the best way to integrate individuals into groups for productive purposes. Always, getting things done for the organization has competed with the needs of people who do the actual work. Since the beginnings of the Industrial Revolution, this tension has been brought into sharp focus. The development of the factory system and bureaucracy, job specialization, scientific and technological progress, and other aspects of modern industrial society have raised enduring issues of how to harmonize the interests of organizations and their employees.

Various visions arise on how to simultaneously create abundance and foster the well-being of individuals. At the heart of them all is the belief that there is an essential unity of interests among people in society and at work. Yet this idea about shared pursuits coexists with a knowledge-based ideology that supports the legitimacy of administrative elites and top-down control of organizations. The paradoxical goal is to create a sense of community within work organizations, while simultaneously allowing some people to have more power than others. This means presuming the knowledge of certain individuals to be superior to—not just different from—that of others. This mindset leads to the misguided notion that the task of creating community, meaning, and achievement in organizations can be engineered or motivated into existence by a privileged few.

The sociology of knowledge—or the opinion that the wisdom of some classes of employees is inherently superior, more valuable, or more legitimate than others—invites people at the top to believe that they have the right to control what happens in organizations and still get good results. However, the centralization of control that supports the knowledge-elite model inevitably is out of touch with the day-to-day work experiences of staff down the line. It produces ever-denser webs of rules to control behavior at the point of production or service, and it is a barrier to high performance. At the bottom, the elitist knowledge model, and the authoritarian management philosophy that inevitably surfaces to support it, is based upon mistrust of the knowhow, motivation, and commitment of employees. To realize trust, organizations must embrace a dramatically different conception of what people have to offer on the job.

This chapter reviews contradictory answers to this problem: responses producing either high-trust or low-trust organizations. High-trust organizations are founded on faith in people and a willingness to let them do their jobs. High-trust organizations strive to realize commitment and "beyond-contract" behavior. Finally, high-trust organizations know that extraordinary performance involves everyone and cannot be manipulated into existence.

Trust and Assumptions About Human Nature

Whether organizations trust people depends upon their cosmology or world view concerning human nature. If it is believed that people instinctively enjoy work, then trust and empowerment follow. If people are expected to be unreliable, lazy, or indifferent about their responsibilities, then they are not trusted with much authority over their jobs.

Wrightsman (1964) has measured various aspects of philosophies of human nature. These bear directly on trust and the extent to which certain organizational methods can be used to control employee behavior. Four are especially relevant in understanding how management philosophies are formed:

1. The degree to which we think people are trustworthy or untrustworthy.

2. The degree to which we believe that people are altruistic or selfish.

3. The degree to which we believe that people are independent and self-reliant or dependent and conformist.

4. The degree to which we believe that people are simple versus highly complex organisms.

The first two assumptions are directly about whether people can be trusted; the latter two say something about how easily people can be controlled. Taken together, the mix of perceptions will drive different kinds of management methods, personnel policies, and work procedures. Some, obviously, are high trust, low control. The others are low trust, high control, and that is what we mostly see in modern institutions.

The clearest, and perhaps most influential, description of managerial assumptions about employees and how they leverage organizational policies was made explicit by Douglas McGregor (1960).

McGregor was fascinated by the developments in the physical sciences of his time in releasing and harnessing atomic energy. He felt that dominant conceptions of human nature then being applied in work organizations were, like the theories of physical sciences predating the discovery of atomic energy, both inadequate and incorrect. He was certain that "under proper conditions, unimagined resources of creative human energy could become available within the organizational setting" if only wrongheaded propositions about human effort at work could be changed (McGregor, 1966, cited in Stillman, 1983, p. 330).

McGregor argued that behind every managerial decision were assumptions about human nature and behavior. The first set of these he labeled as the now-familiar Theory X, which legitimized the idea of top-down direction and control of organizations. These attitudes were that:

1. The average human being has an inherent dislike of work and will avoid it if he can.
2. Because of this human characteristic of dislike of work, most people must be coerced, controlled, directed, threatened with punishment to get them to put forth adequate effort toward the achievement of organizational objectives.
3. The average human being prefers to be directed, wishes to avoid responsibility, has relatively little ambition, wants security above all (McGregor, 1960, pp. 33–34).

As is well known, Theory X is decidedly low trust. However, if one holds these beliefs, there is little cognitive dissonance or need to rationalize imbalances in power relations at work or even question their legitimacy. Further, at the heart of this theory of the "mediocrity of the masses" (p. 34) is the conviction that most people have little experience-based learning or knowledge to contribute to improve organizational performance.

McGregor counterpoised the mistrust-centered Theory X with

a high-trust Theory Y, which proposes very different suppositions about people and work. Three of these are especially interesting and relate directly to the problem and potential of creating high-trust learning organizations. McGregor (1960, p. 48) wrote that:

1. The average human being learns, under proper conditions, not only to accept but to seek responsibility. Avoidance of responsibility, lack of ambition, and emphasis on security are generally consequences of experience, not inherent human characteristics.
2. The capacity to exercise a relatively high degree of imagination, ingenuity, and creativity in the solution of organizational problems is widely, not narrowly, distributed in the population.
3. Under conditions of modern industrial life, the intellectual potentialities of the average human being are only partially utilized.

The thrust of the Theory Y assumptions are, first, that if it is true that people behave poorly at work, it is because they have been taught to do so. Second, creativity, innovation, and high performance are not the exclusive properties of administrative elites. Third, the way organizations are led and managed represses, rather than releases, the full productive energy of individuals. In short, the possibility of a nuclear explosion of productivity in the American workplace was being systematically crushed by the dead weight of self-serving and incorrect assumptions about human nature. These false assumptions have been around since the beginning of the century and continue into the present. They have been lethal for trust.

Working Beyond Contract

High-performing learning organizations have faith in people. They are also aware that they need people to contribute more than what is minimally described in their position descriptions. They appreciate that "I do my job" can easily convey less rather than more. What high-performing, learning organizations require is the difference between what is known as dependable role behavior and such notions as moral involvement (Etzioni, 1961), mutual commitment (Walton, 1987), innovative and spontaneous activity (Katz, 1964), organizational citizenship (Organ, 1988), and prosocial behavior (Brief and Motowidlo, 1986). It means doing more than what is expected, being a "good soldier," giving a helping hand when needed. People who work beyond contract make extraordinary contributions.

An example of beyond-contract behavior occurred recently when a desperate taxpayer walked several miles to Ogden, Utah, thinking that he could get his tax refund check there. The hapless person had gone to the wrong place; his check was in San Francisco. Employees went out of their way to contact San Francisco, get him his badly needed check, and found him food and shelter too (Rivenbark, 1994).

Organizations want employees to work beyond contract, to do more than what is strictly specified. This is because there is a serious difference between complying with authority and willingly, even enthusiastically, volunteering one's services. There is a profound distinction between faithfully following orders and actively seeking opportunities to advance organizational interests. These latter concepts represent a level of dedication beyond just honoring directives. They transcend what command alone can motivate and incentives can induce.

Public executives who rely on rules to prevent employees from exercising discretion because of the belief that they cannot be trusted must learn to let go of this belief; they must give staff greater opportunity to do more than what is just required. It means breaking down the mindset that a knowledge elite can manage change by itself. According to Vice President Gore, for instance, "In the old way of doing things, federal executives were expected to know best, and they created special offices at the top of their organizational chart to manage and create innovation alone" (Rivenbark, 1994, p. 5).

That obviously has to stop. When it does, remarkable things can happen. One example: employees at the New York regional office of Veterans Affairs worked as a team and cut a twenty-three-step process for determining benefits to just eight steps; that reduced processing costs 20 percent and cut client waiting time from thirty minutes to *three* minutes.

Another example is evident in the Occupational Safety and Health Administration office in Cincinnati, where inspectors are given more responsibility for decisions. They can decide to conduct interviews on or off site, during or after work hours. They can even write reports away from their offices as long as they stay in touch with their supervisors. Finally, they manage their own time, set their own goals, and determine when they should take leave. According to their office director, trusting employees has increased both their effectiveness and self-esteem. He says that they have more data to make decisions than he does and "we're giving them maximum latitude in making decisions" (Harris, 1994, p. 12).

These kinds of outcomes are the result of permitting employees greater discretion in doing their jobs by breaking down the boundaries that constrain their actions. They demonstrate what happens when organizations trust employees to do a better job.

Higher-order involvement of the beyond-contract kind means not only being willing to act, but anticipating and searching out opportunities for action. It means being game to take a chance, to risk, to try something new. It means playing with a problem to find a solution. It means, in sum, delivering more than is required and more than what is expected. In the present vernacular, it is not merely satisfying but "delighting" the customer or client.

This is in contrast with constrained low-trust attitudes, which may lead people to work indifferently, regulate their own work behavior in ways that obstruct management purposes, quietly subvert authority or openly challenge it, and totally withhold all spirit of loyalty to, or identification with, the company (Fox, 1974b, pp. 1–2). This "us versus them" outlook promotes attitudes of "it's not in my job description" and "we do our eight and hit the gate."

To get beyond contract, leaders of organizations need to reexamine their fundamental premises about employees. They need to rethink all they have learned about how organizations ought to be administered. That means that they must reject the controlling legacy of scientific management and the too-often manipulative character of the human relations movement. These two are at the heart of the dominant management philosophy operating in most public organizations today.

The Enduring Low-Trust Legacy of Scientific Management

The latter half of the 1880s saw major technological advancements. The capability to standardize parts and work processes led to mass production. Before this time, all aspects of getting a product from conception, to design, into production, and, finally, to a customer were in the hands of artisans and their apprentices. They enjoyed full scope of action in doing work and had direct personal control over their job knowledge. With the growth of large mass production enterprises came the need to develop advanced systems of control. To introduce these modern production systems, the knowhow of staff had to be commandeered.

The introduction of "scientific management" by Frederick W. Taylor in the early twentieth century marks the modern beginning of the recognition of the value of employee work knowledge and the simultaneous attempt to expropriate it for organizational purposes. The goal of scientific management was to establish highly rationalized procedures for rendering work through the use of new techniques of human engineering. The principal idea was to break jobs down into their component parts, observe humans in the accomplishment of tasks, and then connect the two to achieve optimal efficiency. Scientific management took skills from the hands of workers, engineered them, and eventually returned them in the form of highly specialized jobs. People were seen as extensions of technology. Work was dominated and controlled by detailed rules monitored by close supervision. Social subsystems were subordinated to technical systems.

Taylor (1911, pp. 39, 63) outlines the purpose of his scientific method: "The managers assume . . . the burden of gathering together of all the traditional knowledge which in the past has been possessed by the workmen and then of classifying, tabulating, and reducing this knowledge to rules, laws, and formulae. . . . All possible *brain work* [italics added] should be removed from the shop and centered in the planning or laying-out department." Some have argued that this deskilling of labor was intentional, designed to lessen the dependency of owners on workers and to lower wage costs (Braverman, 1974; Perrow, 1986). No matter what the motive, it was based on mistrust of employee commitment to do good work.

Taylor was very suspicious that a great many employees resisted doing all they could to aid production. He observed that many employees were engaged in "soldiering"—intentionally working below their full capacity. He surmised that "the greatest part of systematic soldiering . . . is done by the men with the deliberate object of keeping their employers ignorant of how fast work can be done. So universal is soldiering for this purpose, that hardly a competent workman can be found in a large establishment . . . who does not devote a considerable part of his time to studying just how slowly he can work and still convince his employer that he is going at a good pace" (pp. 32–33).

All this assumed negligence was seen as having a terrible effect on efficiency, which meant, of course, that it had to be stamped out. More to the point, employee discretion had to be eliminated; it was the enemy of efficiency. As Kelman (1987, p. 196) notes, the problem of "irreducible discretion" is still viewed as "some sort of disease" in administration. This low-trust mentality endures in the typical government agency.

Trust and the Lessons of Motivation

The usual response to the damage done by the excessively bureaucratic, scientific, and mass production work model is to rely on motivational strategies to repair things. Motivation, in its simplest form, is positive energy directed toward the achievement of some goal. How it gets started, what sustains it, and what causes it to stop have received considerable attention from organizational researchers over the years. The problem is that, historically, assorted motivational schemes have been sufficiently manipulative to evoke mistrust. Further, the thrust of various motivational methods is grounded in legitimizing the troublesome management ideology that simultaneously espouses a unitary theory of interests while denying the realities of conflict, power, control, and the true situation of the subordinate.

Some employers, for example, try to use motivational methods to substitute for real empowerment. They try to gloss over their century-old low-trust operating premises with techniques that merely try to make employees *feel better* about their conditions, rather than change them. Unfortunately, this has been a recurrent problem with much of what has passed for human relations or humanist endeavors in organizations. In too many cases, they have been nothing more than cynical attempts to manipulate employee emotions when more control-oriented authority methods failed.

The human relations movement grew out of early efforts to use the tools of individual and group psychology for organizational objectives. It correctly recognized organizations as social systems where the quality of social interactions played a significant role in determining individual, group, and organizational performance. It marked a shift in thinking about how organizations should be managed. Trust is a variable that gets a good deal of attention from organizational humanists. The question is whether the notice it receives is based on an interest in manipulating staff compliance solely to legitimize managerial control or to allow all employees the opportunity to have more voice, oversight, and power over their work. The difference is crucial.

The origins and boundaries of the human relations movement are unclear, but most treatments begin with the classic Hawthorne experiments between 1924 and 1932. Researchers discovered that social factors, such as the morale and solidarity of employees, played a significant role in production, and they realized that social and psychological factors needed to be taken into consideration on the job. In fact, the formal organization, so carefully designed and nurtured by the scientific school of management, was found to be less important than maintaining the equilibrium of the informal social system and the collaboration of employees (Roethlisberger and Dickson, 1939). The problem is that "maintaining the equilibrium" was used to serve the high-control, low-trust model of management. The psychology of employees became one more contingency to be dominated.

Chester Barnard, in his significant book *The Functions of the Executive* (1938), encouraged the idea that organizations are social systems and their success depends less on the design of formal authority structures and more on an understanding of how to secure employees' cooperation. For him, trust was at the heart of cooperation. "These structures do not remain in existence, they usually do not come into being, the vitality is lacking, there is no enduring cooperation, without the creation of *faith* [italics added], the catalyst by which the living system of human effort is enabled to continue its incessant interchanges of energies and satisfactions" (p. 259). Faith—or trust—was the stitch that held the social fabric together.

Barnard argued that it is natural for people to cooperate. However, in a somewhat contradictory fashion so typical of the times, he advocated the indoctrination of lower-level employees into such natural behavior and indicated that the "final test" of his "conceptual scheme is whether its use will make possible a more effective conscious promotion and manipulation of co-operation among men" (p. 74).

The Hawthorne experiments and the work of Chester Barnard mark a radical departure from classical organizational theory by shifting focus and attention away from the design of controlling managerial hierarchies, spans of control, impoverished job design, and so on, to a concern with the social-psychological interests of the individual employee. However, issues related to the sociology of knowledge and the power of subordinates over their work are not adequately addressed. It is still believed that superior knowledge rests at the top of organizations and that it is management's responsibility to make sure things get done right. Shared interests are assumed and disparities in power are mostly ignored.

The human relations school was centered in the unitary view of organizations. In this view, the achievement of common objectives is emphasized, conflict is considered a rare and transient phenomenon usually caused by deviants and troublemakers, and the prerogative of guiding the organization toward the achievement of common interests should be ideally in the hands of higher authorities (Morgan, 1986).

As Denhardt (1993, p. 111) observes, despite a shift toward a concern with broader needs of subordinates, "it was clear that the chief objective of the manager (and, not coincidentally, the chief concern of the management scientist) was to find the most efficient way to secure worker compliance with the wishes of management." The central problem concerning trust persisted as the field of human relations developed. Denhardt (1993) captures the essence of the difficulty when he further observes that although the human relations approach appreciates human factors in organizational life, it ultimately treats these as just another set of inducements to be manipulated in the pursuit of managerial control. Where conflicts arise between the individual and the organization, managers are encouraged to fall back on hierarchical authority.

Ruling doctrines do not give in easily to competing conceptualizations. Various maintenance strategies are employed to protect governing beliefs. These strategies include methods to socialize individuals into accepting the preferred reality as inevitable, cooptation designs, therapeutic programs, and, finally, destruction of ideas that are unduly threatening (Berger and Luckman, 1967; Selznick, 1949). Nothing really revolutionary happens. In the work situation, there is only the attempt to integrate staff into the dominant system of knowledge by extending a modest measure of "relative worker autonomy" to deal with the unacceptable problems of job alienation and low commitment arising out of traditional command methods (Edwards, 1979; Hearn, 1988).

When organizations attempt to use unobtrusive control mechanisms made available by behavioral science to achieve the collaboration and control they cannot elicit in other ways, they violate conditions of trust. For example, even in the context of total quality management, there is a tendency to interpret the importance of employee pride in terms of motivation that "causes" better work. This interpretation overlooks the original intent of quality management, which points out that to get quality, organizations must enable people to first feel free to do work well, the result of this freedom being the generator of pride.

Relatedly, as has been suggested by some theories of motivation, we have the cause and effect arrows going the wrong way (Porter and Lawler, 1968). People feel pride and are motivated as a *result* of high performance, not the other way around. In the misinterpretation of this fundamental insight, staff motivation and pride in work continue to be thought of in traditional human relations terms as a way of inducing or manipulating the employee to make the right moves—always, however, according to the blueprints of higher (and presumably more knowledgeable) authorities rather than by establishing institutionalized conditions that release the potential for superior achievement and the trust that will be naturally reciprocated.

The combined legacy of scientific management and the human relations movement fosters a belief that organizations can be dominated or engineered into high performance and employees can be made to feel good about it. It leads to what Vaill (1991) characterizes as the "grand paradox of management"—the belief that managers can overpower what is essentially uncontrollable. This mindset leads to the degenerative physics recognized by McGregor that represses, rather than releases, the productive energy of organizations. The mindset is, if things do not get done as they should, either there is not enough management, analysis, or control or the wrong type of motivational scheme is being used. The notion that there is likely to be too much of these things is rarely entertained. Managers are prone to believe that system failure and low trust must be the fault of employees, not the work processes and organizational climate that have been constructed by their superiors. In response to system failure, they press harder on the control pedal, rather than shift gears to a different operating philosophy.

Confronting the Managerial Barrier

People want to trust co-workers and superiors. They yearn for environments that promote trust rather than ones that engender fear, alienation, wariness, and suspicion. These feelings, after all, take a huge psychological toll on individuals. The U.N.'s International Labor Organization, for instance, reports that job stress is "increasing to the point of a worldwide epidemic" (Associated Press, 1993b, p. 13) and the costs in compensation claims, reduced productivity, absenteeism, added health insurance costs and direct medical expenses for related diseases like high blood pressure and heart attacks total nearly $200 billion yearly in the United States alone.

A major cause of stress for employees in "ordinary jobs," according to the U.N. study, is the pressures arising from eavesdropping and other kinds of close surveillance by employers (Associated Press, 1993b). Other companies are using computer chips in name badges to track the movement of employees. One computer magazine recently reported that more than 20 percent of American companies have searched employee computer files, voice mail, electronic mail, and other network communications. Another recent report said the United States is becoming a "surveillance society" (Associated Press, 1993b).

It cannot be underestimated how many citizens get out of bed in the morning with depressing and crippling emotions that emanate from the low-trust work climates they face as they head off to work.

Employees want to trust that they can take risks, make mistakes, and be authentic without fear of recrimination. They want to sense that they are expected to face the reality of a work situation and will be supported in judging best how to do their jobs. They want confidence shown in their knowledge of the circumstance. A contemporary training film on excellence in the public sector characterizes this feeling as workers wanting to "control or own their piece of the world."

The attitude of many organizational leaders is a barrier to trust. The problem is that many of them have been taught or socialized into confusing it with predictability, compliance, and obedience. Managers have been indoctrinated into the ideology that all necessary learning in a situation can be stabilized, identified, captured, and controlled through engineering and various motivational plans. They are led to believe that the right moves are discoverable and the rules, regulations, standard operating procedures, and policies they rely upon are reliable in the face of nearly every imaginable contingency. These are the attitudes that need to be changed.

New forms of work design and fresh roles for managers are starting to be described. Organizations are encouraged to be more organic and flexible. They are told to flatten hierarchies and empower subordinates. Managers are summoned to abandon their command and control orientation and adopt new roles as coaches, facilitators, teachers, mentors, builders of learning systems, and entrepreneurs. They are encouraged to create a new world of work characterized by continuous learning, quality, teamwork, and empowered employees. There is a collision of paradigms, a time warp between the world of mass production values and the post-modern organization. The contemporary manager is caught in the middle of this change.

The traditional (and still dominant) managerial model of work makes it difficult for managers to trust change. Ultimately, they are still responsible when things go wrong. In contemporary times executives have legitimate fears that the slightest mistake can cost them their careers. They hear about empowerment and high performance, but they see the empty desks and know their job security is always on the line. They know that part-time, temporary work awaits even those with superior skills and dedication. If they lose their jobs, there are not many places to go any more. Perhaps it is not control they crave, but safety. They rightly ask, if they risk empowerment or expanding the scope of action of their subordinates, who will pay the price if something goes wrong?

A military officer captured the dilemma well. When a free thinker tries new things, he noted, the odds are that mistakes will be made and one "oh, no" will wipe out a thousand "atta boys." Moreover, he said, when an officer fails at an important task by using conventional methods, it will be excused as a failure due to overwhelming odds or to circumstances beyond the officer's control. If the same officer fails while trying something new, there is no such excuse and the prevailing attitude will be "why didn't the stupid [expletive deleted] do it the way he was supposed to?"

Perhaps we have misunderstood or undervalued why managers are barriers to high performance. A lot of them do have trouble sharing power or listening to all the noise that empowerment brings. But this is uncharted territory for most of them. They are acting on what they know and what they have been taught. The more senior of them learned that earlier innovations in management philosophy were ideological and short term. Not much of consequence was really going to change. As Applebaum and Batt (1994, p. 12) note, "Work reform was viewed as a tactical tool for improving workers' attitudes and job satisfaction. The emphasis was on motivation, and workers rarely had the discretion or authority to alter the production process or have a say in how the gains were to be distributed." These reforms were transitory tactics to solve some immediate crisis. They did not challenge the fundamental logic of the bureaucratic, mass production system and were not an integral part of a strategy to help organizations reposition themselves to respond to new organizational performance criteria.

In short, the rhetoric and change strategies did have effects, but they were fleeting. Managers knew where they stood and were confident that, in the long run, the way their organizations operated would stay essentially the same. Nothing fundamental was going on. That is not the case any more and managers—particularly middle managers—are beginning to pay a real price in terms of their careers.

General management is in some real degree of trouble in contemporary organizations. We have developed two new heroes in the emerging world of work. The first is the visionary leader at the top of the organization (the leader hero), and the second is all those who toil at the point of production and service (the working-class hero). We celebrate their arrival and encourage their development. We seem to ignore the fact that everyone is going to have to play some role as change agent if we are going to realize real change. That means that managers, executives, supervisors, and administrators have a part to play too. Rather than handle them with a measure of respect, we have made them the villains in the piece. No wonder they are defensive. Whom do they have to trust?

Everything we know about organizational change and development tells us that people cannot change, will not change, unless they are afforded some measure of psychological safety. Until managerial needs are respected and addressed, permanent change will come hard, if at all.

Creating Conditions for Change

It is important to understand that problems of higher-order dedication are everyone's problem. Predicaments of trust are not necessarily more consequential at one level of an organization than another. Systems reflect myriad interdependencies and dynamic complexity. Every person's attitude ultimately influences performance.

Recently I consulted with a public hospital stressed about its chances for survival in an increasingly unstable and competitive health care market. The hospital has initiated a quality improvement program. I dealt primarily with the nursing staff. They are seen as key in improving customer service through their attention to patient care. However, a caring attitude toward patients can be wholly subverted if the billing department does its job poorly, if the admissions people are indifferent, if the rooms, corridors, or cafeteria appear dirty, or if the physicians do not communicate well with families. Organizations are systems—period. Fixing a piece of them does not produce much when it comes to high performance. In the case of trust, how people feel everywhere in the system is consequential. Therefore, the challenge of achieving trust and the meaningful involvement of people exists at every tier.

It is clear that there can be very profound complicating factors that interfere with building trust in organizations. For instance, from the perspective of the executive fearful of losing a job, trust can be the beginning of a road to disaster. In the case of employees, expressions of trust raise expectations and faith in their freedom to be authentic and have greater oversight of the conception and execution of their work. One party is trying to constrain scope of action while the other is attempting to enlarge it. Both wish to survive. Where there is a discrepancy in motive or intent between groups, the trust connection is missed.

In fact, problems of trust worsen, and that is what is happening in many organizations today. Weisbord (1987) suggests that it is the people in the middle that we ought to help lead the change to more productive, dignified, and meaningful work communities. After all, they have the most to lose, and these previously loyal people deserve a better role than rejection, a week's notice, and an outplacement counselor waiting in the next room.

Several things should now be clear. First, creating trust in organizations is critical because it is the major *intangible* factor that influences useful learning.

Second, trust flees force and cannot be commanded into existence. There is always a measure of discretion present in every job, which can be invested or withheld for organizational purposes and which exists beyond the absolute control of authorities. Such beyond-contract behavior is voluntarily granted.

Third, rousing trust is important at every level because there is valuable knowledge throughout organizations that is required for high performance. It takes everyone's commitment to change organizations. The current tendency to identify leaders and front-line workers as the only heroes in the battle to achieve high performance is a mistake. Such a perspective is overworked in the popular literature on organizational transformation. It breeds fear and defensiveness among middle managers and front-line supervisors and makes them reluctant to embrace necessary change.

Fourth, trust cannot be manipulated into existence. Trust is an attitude that is voluntarily granted to others only after assessing whether the recipients are worthy of such consideration. It is *built* through countless exchanges conducted over time between people where each has something to offer or withhold, and whose conduct is appraised by the other for indications of motive and reliability. It demands authenticity. The use of the word *built* in conjunction with trust is meant to underscore the care with which this attitude is constructed, as opposed to commanded or orchestrated. An equally appropriate word is *earned*, which also implies the slow accumulation of this precious capital. In contemporary organizations, building trust starts with leadership.

PART TWO

Keys to Building Trustworthy Organizations

4

Trustworthy Leadership: Helping People to Lead Themselves

It starts at the top. Though the payoffs of trust arise from all the processes of work in organizations, leadership is the absolutely essential factor in building conditions of faith and confidence in organizations.

A new point about leadership needs to be made and understood. We are not dealing with the traditional organization when it comes to trust and high performance. We are not confronting a situation where leaders can just order things to happen or rely on simple inducements to get results. We are not seeking to establish heroes at the top who are wiser than anyone else and are depended upon for the answers. The high-performing organization insists on a different type of leadership. In a sentence: *The goal of all leadership in high-performing organizations is to reduce subordinate dependency and build self-leadership among individual workers and teams.* This theory of high-trust leadership means unlearning some of the basic assumptions about how to lead that have been embedded in traditional bureaucratic organizations.

Leaders are typically most influential when it comes to the management philosophy and nature of work processes that are instituted within an organization. Effective leaders recognize that trust is indispensable for the well-being of their organizations and the people who work in them. More than anything else, when it comes to building trust, the most impressive leadership helps people gain greater competence and self-control when doing their work.

High-trust leadership means letting go of explicit controls and substituting implicit norms to guide individual behavior. It requires inspiring people rather than forcing performance. The leader's primary role in the high-performing organization is creating conditions where "people are continually expanding their capabilities to shape their future—that is, leaders are responsible for learning" (Senge, 1990, p. 9). The high-trust leadership approach is based on positive assumptions about people; it assumes that average people, given half a chance, want to learn and make things better for themselves and their organizations.

The first report of the Winter Commission, which was established to evaluate how to improve the public service in state and local government, echoes this call for a new type of public leader. Under its "trust and lead" strategy, the commission asserts that administrators must "forgo the supervising, disciplining, second-guessing and double-checking that have for so long passed for leadership and begin the coaching, benchmarking, listening, mentoring, and championing that new times and a new type of job-motivated employee demand" (National Commission on the State and Local Public Service, 1993, p. 45). The new role for leaders is to teach workers to trust their own skills and abilities and then get out of their way so they can do their jobs. What is needed in the high-performing organization is the so-called *unleader*, the person who builds capacities in others.

A threshold question arises whether or not there is a difference between leaders and managers. Typically, it is believed that people can be leaders without being managers and that people can manage without being leaders. The term *leader* is used here to mean a person who is involved in change, while managers are perceived as people who pay attention to routines and maintain stability, order, and the status quo. The leader is often engaged in creating chaos while the manager is busy trying to bring it under control. The distinction is admittedly arbitrary. Both change and stability are needed in organizations and there is no doubt that some individuals can create both conditions. It is fair to say, however, that the contemporary problem in many public organizations is that they are overmanaged and underled.

Leaders and Trust

In the stories and sagas of organizations, there are leaders who are talked about long after they have departed. They are remembered for keeping their word, honoring agreements, looking out for the people who worked for them, caring about citizens, talking truth to power, and modeling the behavior they expected from others. They helped people to develop their potential. They were champions of learning. Invariably, they helped to change things for the better. When they left, they prepared others to take their place. These individuals are both exceptional and rare.

Other leaders destroy both trust and high performance. They are driven by personalized power motives (McClelland, 1975). They use influence methods to make situations more favorable for themselves, even if it comes at the expense of other people and the long-term interests of their organizations. They express power in self-aggrandizing ways and exhibit impulsive aggressiveness. They like their name on the door. They manipulate people, overvalue personal loyalty, and are very big on control. They represent the unrestrained narcissistic personality. They assume an "I lead, you follow" posture based on their assumed superior knowledge of what is required at work. They are unable to rely on trust and are often seen as threatening. Subordinates spend a lot of time trying to figure out ways to protect themselves from such individuals.

Leaders with socialized power motives use trust to achieve work conditions that truly legitimize the broader interests of employees and citizens. Their power drive is inhibited and enlisted in the service of others (McClelland, 1975). Their approach is based on positive assumptions about human nature. They treat people like adults. Their theories of action aim to reduce organizational defensive routines, which impair learning (Argyris, 1993). They trust the knowledge that people have and let them use it. They know that employees can contribute to the larger picture. Most important, if they find individuals, groups, or organizations with limited promise or a low sense of efficacy, they help move them forward to higher levels of accomplishment. In the words of one leader, "If you're going to be in an [organization] of any size, you're going to have to develop the kind of leadership qualities that allow you to attract good people, guide them, encourage them, and ultimately trust them—and let them go and do their jobs. Oh, sure, you have to take deep breaths occasionally. But, mostly you have to trust them" (Kouzes and Posner, 1987, p. 147).

The centrality of trust has been identified time and again in what makes leaders and their organizations effective. The relationship between trust and successful leadership styles or ways to influence or enable the behavior of followers is undeniable. The evolution of understanding about how leadership works is underpinned by trust. The argument is always the same. High-trust methods of leadership are more likely to guarantee a leader's success. Stated differently, without capitalizing upon trust, prospects for leader and organizational accomplishment are reduced.

How people feel about human nature *and* the importance of realizing goals is at once predictive of how much they trust and will tend to lead. The intersecting principle underlying many leadership theories is the more leaders have faith and confidence in the ability and attitude of followers, the more they ought to move away from autocratic, directive behavior and the more they should enable people to do their jobs. In other words, leaders should start out with the presumption that mature people will work hard given half a chance. Further, they should have confidence that mature employees know something about work that is invaluable to organizational performance.

Moving from Transactional to Transformational Leadership

There are two basic forms of leadership: transactional and transformational. Transactional leadership involves recognizing what rewards followers want and providing it to them when merited. Transformational leadership entails motivating subordinates to perform beyond what is expected or rising above their own self-interests for higher purposes (Bass, 1985). Transformational leadership is what Burns (1978) equates with moral leadership, where "one or more persons engage with others in such a way that leaders and followers raise one another to higher levels of motivation and morality" (p. 20).

Both forms of leadership can engender trust. The argument here is that the transformational kind holds more promise for creating trust *if* the leader is motivated by socialized power concerns. If not, I want to emphasize, there is a dark side to transformational leadership, and especially the charisma that often accompanies it, that actually promotes subordinate dependency and mistrust.

Transactional leaders primarily appeal to the self-interest of subordinates and treat leadership as a series of utilitarian exchanges or bargains. It is not so much leadership as it is deal making. Followership is based on gaining material rewards and avoiding penalties. The transactional leader, through coaching and similar supportive behavior, helps followers overcome obstacles in their environment and "provides opportunities for growth and development in the form of challenging tasks and opportunities to work under conditions of autonomy" (House, Woycke, and Fodor, 1988, p. 99).

Transactional leadership does create a measure of trust by honoring the bargain or contract between an individual and the organization. It also shows faith in people's ability to do good work. It permits employees to negotiate roles and to have voice in establishing goals and the means to achieve them. Management by objective (MBO) or path-goal approaches to supervision are examples of how this might work in practice. There is nothing wrong with this approach, though it may be limited in its power to inspire high performance.

Utilitarian-based transactional leadership will certainly produce dependable role behavior. However, its ability to cause moral involvement or spontaneous and innovative conduct is restricted because it does not connect with the deeper, psychological needs of followers. It does not arouse the emotions of subordinates that hearten extraordinary performance or beyond-contract behaviors. It does not encourage the same kinds of risks or sacrifices that transformational leadership can. It is not recognized as a powerful intervention strategy to encourage change. People rarely run through a wall for a transactional leader.

Transformational leadership enjoys considerable notice and an almost evangelical popularity because of its facility to promote involvement, ownership, and empowerment among staff. The basic premise is that organizational performance can be uplifted by permitting followers to have real power over their jobs. However, the special quality of transformational leadership is that it does not appeal just to external motivators. Nor does it target dependable role behavior as its primary goal. It is after much more. It is based on shared vision and relies on intrinsic motivation to get people to perform well beyond expectations.

Transformational leaders overhaul the entire culture of an organization. They can create the learning organization. That is the upside. The downside is that it can foster dependency. It can be a hustle. It can disable trust. Like motivation, it cannot encourage trust if it is unauthentic and does not truly commission labor processes that permit people to have more control over their work lives. This is true, of course, of all leadership approaches. The transformational technique gets special consideration here because of its increasing popularity and the extraordinarily strong claims made about its ability to empower subordinates and to create conditions of trust. At the same time, it is worth examining closely because it also reinforces the perhaps false idea that leadership alone can enhance trust and high performance in organizations.

More and more, prescriptions for improving organizations center on transformational or charismatic leadership patterns. These approaches invariably feature the thought that the leader exercises authority, not necessarily by logic, nor by position in any hierarchy, but primarily by personal attributes that appeal to and attract followers. Max Weber's decades-old definition captures the essence of this quality: "'Charisma' shall be understood to refer to an *extraordinary* quality of a person, regardless of whether this quality is actual, alleged, or presumed. 'Charismatic authority,' hence, shall refer to a rule over men, whether predominantly external or predominantly internal, to which the governed submit because of their belief in the extraordinary quality of the specific *person*" (Gerth and Mills, 1946, p. 295). The charismatic connection between leader and follower is emotional and produces unusual commitment.

Research into charismatic and transformational types describes them as possessing vision and a sense of mission. Typically, their vision involves radically changing the status quo. They are able to communicate their views clearly. They empower followers, who are then motivated into action to change their conditions (Conger, 1988). Taking risks, working cultural symbols, establishing unusual levels of trust through personal example and unconventional behavior are typical actions of charismatic leaders (Burns, 1978; Bass, 1985; Bennis and Nanus, 1985)

I once worked for a person who led a large, independent public employee organization. He had previously been manager of a large subsidiary of a major corporation, and was brought in to bring the labor organization out of crisis. He hired good people, listened to what they had to say, and pretty much let them do their jobs. He handed out bonuses and other benefits to each division head who successfully achieved one of the goals or major objectives specified in the organization's massive and largely incomprehensible program budget.

Soon the organization did begin to make strides. There was even the emergence of teamwork at the administrative level. It was all quite orderly. The leader could be trusted to keep his word and honor bargains. He had no malice toward anyone. There was a climate of trust, a sense of security, a modest energy level, and respectable organizational accomplishment. But there was almost no vision. We existed to get the work done, to respond to the membership, to satisfy the board of directors, and to meet our ordinary responsibilities. There was no passion about changing the conditions of workers in any fundamental way. Things just quietly hummed along.

I left this organization to join up with one of the country's largest and noisiest public employee unions. It was a different kind of place with a different kind of leader. Known as "labor's last angry man," he was very much a transformational leader. By sheer force of personality, he had taken an institution of some 250,000 members to more than a million strong. New members were coming in at more than a thousand a week and the organization was changing the face of public-sector employee relations everywhere it went. There was a vision based on the idea that public employees ought to have the right to be recognized for the purpose of collective bargaining—at that time, a radical notion. The union was not only transforming itself, but also enacting rather than just responding to its operating environment.

There was a strong, emotional attachment to the leader. People would refer to him by his first name only—usually in reverent and adoring tones. Some staff feared him, but the members had no doubts. They trusted that he would say anything or do anything on their behalf. In return, the membership would back him up and was always ready for a fight. The place was tumultuous and high performing. It was perpetually in action. It roared along.

These two examples demonstrate the difference in *feel* between transactional and transformational leadership. Both kinds engender trust, though at very different levels. The transformational kind is regularly more dynamic and emotionally charged and can induce higher energy and performance than transactional leadership. It simply has more horsepower.

The substantial research on transformational leadership has

produced impressive empirical findings. House, Woycke, and Fodor (1988), in summarizing much of this research, report that leaders who are seen by followers as transformational are perceived as better managers; considered "great" or "world class"; have higher-performing teams in management simulation exercises; have subordinates who report extra effort, greater work satisfaction, and better organizational effectiveness; and generate higher-performing work groups. Followers of such leaders are more self-assured, describe their work as more meaningful, work longer hours, and report higher trust. It is no wonder that executive development programs that promise transformational skills are a growth industry.

Despite the enthusiasm for this leadership style, one question remains: are there any hazards in relying too much on transformational leadership, or for that matter on any single pattern of leadership?

The Dark Side of Transformational Leadership

One aspect that does not get enough attention in the increasingly popular treatments of transformational and charismatic leadership is the unhealthy dependency they can foster. Another aspect not sufficiently examined is the problem of the staying power of highly personalized leadership. What happens when the leader is no longer around? What can people trust then? The telling issue of how much subordinate capacity is really built by some so-called transformational leaders is worth thinking about when it comes to trust.

A third concern: more notice should be given to the dangers that arise when people try to adopt leadership styles that are not their own. Too many people are attending executive development seminars and consuming self-help books these days in an effort to master charismatic-based styles of leadership. If this particular style does not fit with their personality, they end up faking an approach that is not their own. Employees spot this, and the "leader" loses trust. Too often, such programs merely alter people's language— their espoused theory—rather than how they actually operate.

When that happens, they end up looking superficial and unauthentic, which is destructive of trust. They fail to realize that some very noncharismatic leaders build both great organizations and trust. They also fail to understand that the relationship between some transformational leaders and their followers can be pathological.

Transformational leaders are associated with change. They often emerge in times of chaos or threat. In conventional terms, they are in high demand because of the turbulent operating domains of modern organizations where social, political, technological, legal, and economic contingencies are in constant flux. Transformational leaders display constancy in the face of profound change. They appear stable and even eager to intervene in situations others see as hopeless. Often, they are heroic figures. Followers are relieved by their emergence at such moments and are ready to trust and follow them. Why is this? What is it that arises from the same set of events that produces a sense of crisis in followers and a feeling of opportunity in the leader?

Charismatic leaders, recently labeled transformational, are often permanent outsiders. They have almost no stake in the status quo. It constrains them; it interferes with their vision. Unlike the followers, it is usually not their world that is falling apart. Transformational leaders are permanently disengaged. That is why they are so calm. They have nothing to lose, and their followers usually have everything to lose. There is no shared fear and desperation between the leader and followers. If there were, the leader could not function. As Zalenznik (1977, p. 74) notes, leaders "work in organizations, but they never belong to them."

Hanfstängl's description of Adolf Hitler's ability to connect with the hidden passions, resentments, and longings of a crowd so he could exploit them is an example of how the negative charismatic moves outside the group, reads its mood, and then uses it for his own purposes (quoted in Bullock, 1962, pp. 373–374):

> [He] responds to the vibrations of the human heart with the delicacy of a seismograph, or perhaps of a wireless receiving

set, enabling him, with a certainty with which no conscious gift could endow him, to act as a loudspeaker proclaiming the most secret desires, the least admissible instincts, the sufferings, and personal revolts of a whole nation. . . . [He] enters a hall, he sniffs the air. For a moment he gropes, feels his way, senses the atmosphere. Suddenly he bursts forth. His words go like an arrow to their targets, he touches each private wound on the raw, liberating the mass unconscious, expressing its innermost aspirations, telling it what it most wants to hear.

There is nothing inherently wrong in a person's ability to be detached enough to see opportunities that others cannot conceptualize. That is what innovation and vision are all about. In many respects, one could argue that there is never enough of that capacity around. Max Weber suggested that it was precisely the charismatic types who would counteract the worst tendencies of bureaucratic organizations and rescue people from the "iron cage" they represented (Denhardt, 1993). Given the normal fears most people have about change, it is not surprising that it takes an outsider to see the possibilities in seemingly desperate situations. So, what is the problem?

The problem is that people can come to trust the leader rather than themselves; some so-called transformational leaders encourage the practice. They deceive and, by focusing on other people's fears and weaknesses, create dependency. Rather than rely on what they know, followers can excessively conform to the leader's views. They can deny the truth of their own experiences and make themselves willingly dependent upon the seductive fantasies imposed on them by another.

There is a deep psychological transference that occurs among individuals and crowds in such cases, and it is not entirely healthy (Hummel 1974; Lindbloom, 1990). Devotion to a leader "born of distress and enthusiasm," to use Max Weber's poignant phrase (Gerth and Mills, 1946, p. 249), is anything but empowering. Followers are not really entrusted at all—except to move in the direction they are pointed. In an organization, their true ownership over their work lives is illusory. What the leader knows and says is most determinant, not what subordinates understand.

Things may improve for the followers of charismatic types as long as the leader is around. However, in case after case, the house of cards comes tumbling down when the leader departs or, in some instances, even when the leader is still present. What is eventually discovered is that no enduring capacity has been created for the staff or the organization. People are left exhausted and sometimes worse off than before. They have learned very little about how to effectively confront and resolve challenges by themselves. Not a lot of genuine learning has occurred. Or, if it has, the effects of empowerment can easily be negated if the next leader does not use a leadership style that recognizes and builds upon the staff's newly developed capabilities. The problem, in these situations, is that followers have trusted too much.

The issue of how much trust is adequate in work organizations and political systems is important when it comes to leadership. While there are numerous negative consequences of mistrust, choosing to trust can also be pathological. Deutsch (1958, p. 278) defines when too much trust is dysfunctional. It is when trusting choices "may reflect a compulsive, incorrigible tendency to act in a trusting manner without regard to the characteristics of the situation in which the behavior is to take place. Our everyday language uses terms like 'gullible,' 'credulous,' 'dupe,' and 'self-deception' . . . [to describe such behavior]."

There is a point of diminishing returns with trust, and it starts at the point where independent thinking gives way to naiveté or where a person's faith in others is so uncritically granted that exploitation is possible. Barber (1983) maintains that a measure of healthy skepticism or rational distrust should always be present in individuals, groups, and organizations. This ability to think critically is necessary when it comes to the assurances of leadership, especially when what is being peddled promises empowerment, liberation of the cognitive abilities of staff, and growth through learning.

The test of genuine transformational leadership is whether or not it gives employees the training and authority they need to manage their own jobs, involves them in decisions, provides chances to be part of teams, and commissions those teams to have real power. Another way of examining the authenticity of transformational leadership is to ask whether it builds capacity rather than dependency among subordinates. The kind of leader who cares about trust seeks to develop other leaders throughout the organization. The high-trust leader knows that leadership is indeed a reciprocal influence process where followers, as well as the leader, have an important part to play. The actions of the high-trust leader are aimed at promoting conditions where mutual influence is enabled.

Manfred F. R. Kets de Vries (1993, p. 177) supplies a useful set of questions that, if answered in the affirmative, give definite reasons to worry about whether a leader is having a healthy effect on an organization. They are:

1. Is there a lack of realism in the leader's vision?
2. Does the leader fail to accept personal responsibility for his mistakes?
3. Do people in the organization find themselves forced into self-censorship because of the leader's adverse reactions to bad news?
4. Does she need to be constantly in the limelight?
5. Is she obsessed by her public image?
6. Have suspicion and distrust crept into the organization?

Trust begins to end with transformational/charismatic leadership at precisely the point these dark-side behaviors begin. That is why critical judgment by followers is always in order.

Creating Conditions for Self-Leadership

There are substitutes, supplements, and enhancers that can positively moderate or mediate the effects of leadership, and they can

be systematically created (Kerr, 1977). For instance, a high-performing work team does not need much leadership at all. People in
a close-knit, cohesive work group do not require a supportive or
relationship-oriented leader. If the team or group is competent, it
does not require a great deal of task-related behavior either. The
group is its own leader (Manz, 1986).

Leadership in a team environment is different. The idea is to
develop people who are self-motivated. These leaders get things
done not by hoarding power and responsibility but by handing it
out to others. For them, power is not a zero-sum game. They are, in
fact, what some have called the "unleaders," those who aim to
develop others to lead themselves (Manz and Sims, 1984).

Many individuals are their own leaders. People do possess internal self-control systems, and those explain, in part, how people
behave. To comprehend high performance as a direct or sole function of outside-in, top-down leadership of any variety is just plain
limiting.

Increasingly, there is elevated interest in theories of self-leadership, which relies on the naturally motivating potential of the
intrinsic value of task performance. Manz (1986) connects this idea
to what is known about self-efficacy. His theory is that, as people's
feelings of self-efficacy increase, the better they perform. These feelings have a reciprocal relationship with performance: the better
people perform the more self-efficacy they experience, and so on.
The sense of elevated efficacy comes from feedback in doing the
work itself. As we know from the relationship between views of
human nature and how they influence both motivation and leadership methods, trust in people is the triggering element in such
physics.

The idea that hierarchical leadership is not the only—or even
the most important—factor in influencing relationships, attitudes,
and behaviors on the job has been recognized for a long time (Kerr
and Jermier, 1978). Contingency and situational theorists, for
instance, argue that characteristics of the subordinate (ability, experience, training), of the task (clarity, identity, significance, feed-

back), and of the organization (extent of formalization, nature of the reward system, task interdependencies) also matter. Situations can be structured in ways that create trust independent of the personal style of any leader. In the long run, it is how rules, roles, and relations are institutionalized that are telling when it comes to trust and high performance. A transformational leader, for instance, could not use inspiration to overcome work structures that systematically undercut or destroy trust. The elements of the work system become a "leadership neutralizer"—something that makes it impossible for the leader to succeed (Howell, Dorfman, and Kerr, 1986). Ultimately, the essence of the overall work program will assert itself. It will either sustain or undercut trust.

Systems thinking is antithetical to the idea that any single contingency can explain how trust and high performance are actually built in organizations. Therefore, people's faith and focus should be in bettering the general quality of work arrangements and not just the personal attributes of individual leaders—even if those are occasionally quite exceptional. Leadership is one factor, albeit an important one, but not the sole ingredient necessary for creating conditions of trust.

Surmounting leadership and the dependence it fosters is a somewhat radical idea in our culture, where leadership is so highly prized. As Gibb (1978, p. 260) notes, "The transcendence of leadership and the building of processes that do not depend upon leadership are doorways to higher states of being, to greater fulfillment, and to higher levels of productivity and spirituality. A crucial step in the growth of the person is the movement away from dependence upon the leadership of another person. The key to the future lies in increasing the number of instances of emergent leaderless groups in education, business, therapy and all phases of life." The key to changing environmental quality is the growing trust in ourselves *as individuals* and also *as groups and communities*.

Leadership is also a reciprocal process, at least partly dependent upon the willingness of followers to be led. It is not a one-way street. However, rather than concentrate so much on how to make the leadership end of the process work better, we would more effectively build trust if we paid more attention to the other end—the followers. It is time to concentrate on strengthening the opportunities of followers to learn how to motivate, organize, and control their own activities. The result is a more powerful and cohesive work community.

High-Trust Leadership Methods

There are several theories of leadership, but as yet no general theory of leadership that integrates various conceptual frameworks has been developed (Yukl, 1994). However, certain themes are common in these frameworks, themes that suggest specific ways that leaders can use their influence to increase trust in organizations.

1. *Increase feeling of self-efficacy.* The key activity of high-trust leadership is developing greater self-leadership capacities and feelings of self-efficacy among followers. Self-efficacy makes individuals and groups (collective self-efficacy) believe they can accomplish great feats. As self-efficacy increases, so does the amount of effort and persistence employed to attain goals (Bandura, 1986). Mistrust dissipates feelings of self-efficacy. Mistrust is created by leaders motivated by excessive self-interest, a lack of genuine concern for others, and a tendency to use power to manipulate and control people for their own purposes.

2. *Create shared vision.* One persistent theme in studies of leadership is the importance of shared vision. The idea of vision suggests the ability to perceive alternative futures that are more appealing than present reality. Vision implies change. It is, as one observer noted, a target that beckons. The question concerning trust is, whose vision is it that invites organizational change? Or, more accurately, whose vision *should* it be?

Leadership, like trust, is a reciprocal process where both leaders and followers have important roles to play. This means that the leader informs and is informed about what the organization ought to be doing. Ideally, any vision concerning the future is arrived at by everyone who has a stake in that future. Successful visions in large, mature organizations (so typical in the public sector) evolve over long periods of time and are the product of participative processes. The leader's role is promoting mutual respect and trust among all members. This means listening, modeling tolerance of different points of view, and establishing credibility.

Powerful visions are firmly rooted in the values and desires of the group. When Martin Luther King, for example, said "I have a dream" it was deeply connected with the goals of his followers. It embodied their most cherished hopes and aspirations. It mirrored their desires and that is why the vision worked to bind Dr. King and his followers together in a powerful emotional way.

On the other hand, building shared vision is a behavior that "dark-side" transformational or excessively self-interested leaders do not seem to be able to practice or sustain over time. They have too much confidence in their own vision and not much genuine faith in the views of other people. Their need for the adulation of followers makes them unable to maintain the cooperative relationships that create shared vision, mutual trust, and community (Yukl, 1994). They appeal to followers' weaknesses, not their strengths.

Leaders who cannot communicate their vision clearly have trouble with trust, as President Bush did, for instance, with his seeming inability to come to terms with the "vision thing." President Carter also had a vision for the nation but he too had problems articulating it.

3. *Concentrate on tasks and relationships.* Emphasizing tasks means concentrating on getting the job done. Attention to relationships means showing concern for subordinates. Studies of leadership show that effective leaders demonstrate at least a moderate level of concern for both tasks and relationships. These two values sometimes compete and often are in conflict. Nonetheless, effec-

tive leaders are able to find a way to balance these objectives. A leader who is unable to deal with a dual concern for both tasks and relationships runs the risk of losing the trust of followers. It is difficult to trust a leader who is not competent or attentive when it comes to getting the work done. Followers are also not likely to trust a leader who does not seem to care what happens to the people in the organization.

4. *Use power to discourage dependency*. Leadership research also shows that negative charismatics or transformational leaders with personalized power motives tend to run afoul of trust. At first they may seem charming and sincerely concerned for the welfare of others, but over time their real lack of positive regard for others usually becomes apparent and causes interpersonal problems with subordinates. Personal power charismatics "seek to dominate and subjugate followers by keeping them weak and dependent on the leader. Authority for making important decisions is centralized in the leader, rewards and punishments are used to manipulate and control followers, and information is restricted and used to maintain the image of leader infallibility or to exaggerate external threats to the organization" (Yukl, 1994, p. 334). These behaviors are antithetical to trust.

5. *Create a healthy learning environment*. Effective leaders perform coaching, teaching, and mentoring roles in their organizations. These leaders know the importance of both individual and organizational learning. They enable and help guide the process of learning rather than dictate it. They work on their own skills and provide developmental opportunities for others. Effective leaders seek to truly empower and elevate followers by activating their higher-order needs and moral values (Burns, 1978). This pattern of behavior helps people lift themselves up and positions them to have greater self-confidence and self-management ability. It also makes them less dependent on the leader.

6. *Be consistent*. Constructive leadership communicates effec-

tively and behaves consistently. Leaders who shift positions frequently also undermine trust and subvert follower commitment. For instance, President Clinton's behavior during the 1992 campaign seemed to invite problems of trust when he was accused of constantly "flip-flopping" on issues. Establishing trust through consistency is evidenced by President Reagan's strategy of "staying the course" even when his policies seemed not to be working. No matter what people thought about the president's agenda, they were clear about where he stood and where he was headed, and that is more assuring for trust.

7. *Work on culture.* Competent leaders change organizations by paying serious attention to organizational culture—the values, beliefs, and assumptions shared by members of an organization. Culture is an organization's personality or learned responses to problems of survival. According to Schein (1992), leaders can have significant impact on shaping an organization's culture, by what they pay attention to, how they react to crises, whether they model the kind of behavior they expect from others, how they use rewards to reinforce what is important, and the kinds of people they recruit and the criteria they employ to expel people from the organization. Each of these things is closely monitored by subordinates and can be done in ways that help or hurt trust relations at work. Actions speak louder than words in organizations; what leaders do, as opposed to what they say, is most telling when it comes to trust.

8. *Integrate practices.* The leadership challenge in creating high-trust organizations, finally, means establishing processes that reduce defensive routines and free the experiential knowledge of employees. This involves creating an entire system of mutually reinforcing high-trust work practices that encourage self-motivation and self-leadership. These practices include, at a minimum, guaranteeing participation, opening communication, being fair, guaranteeing due process, and establishing opportunities for individual development. These dynamics must be supported by a human resources management system that is in synch with these ideals.

Creating such systems is not easy. It requires constant attention and continuing effort to support people's ability to lead themselves and sustain ownership of their work. And it is not something that can be done overnight. It defies the quick fix. What leaders pay attention to, how they react in a crisis, the kinds of behavior they model, and, generally, their reputation for fairness and integrity are the actions that build trust over the long haul. The next step is getting people involved.

5

Creating Participation and Involvement

Opportunities to participate increase trust in organizations. Participatory work cultures also facilitate learning (Watkins and Marsick, 1993).

Thus an organization's willingness to use participative processes, to involve people in decision making, is the primary way of building trust, learning, and high performance.

Participation is democratic. It is a way to decentralize authority and influence in an organization. It fosters efficacy, the feeling that organizational change is possible and that individuals can play a role in bringing about this change. According to Nachmias (1985, pp. 137–138), the efficacy-trust connection works this way: "Success in one's attempts to influence changes in the organization increases one's sense of bureaucratic efficacy, and this in turn, increases one's trust in the organization. Conversely, failure to influence decisions through participation leads to a lower sense of bureaucratic efficacy which, in turn, leads to low trust."

Participation grants employees more control over their work lives. Behavioral scientists stress a complementary link between participatory arrangements and cooperative behavior, commitment to an organization's goals, greater trust in managers, and a sense of goodwill toward other organizational members (Levine and Tyson, 1990). Participation gives people more opportunities to communicate, handle conflict, and develop their interpersonal and problem-solving skills. Organizations can expect better decisions and stronger employee commitment to decision implementation. In recognition of these connections, the most frequent innovation initiated in organizations during the 1980s incorporated some form of employee participation (Kochan, Cutcher-Gershenfeld, and MacDuffie, 1989).

Involving employees means trusting them with increased information, power, authority, and responsibility over how work is performed (Mishra and Morrissey, 1990). There are elaborate typologies of participation. In its basic form, however, *participation is about who decides, and how.* Significantly, it concerns whether people will have the chance to engage in the social interactions that encourage incidental or informal learning—the sort of learning upon which much of high performance is based.

Embracing participation to improve organizational performance is further acknowledgment that top-down management cannot keep pace with changing demands on its own. It also shows recognition that low-trust strategies of tight control suppress creative ideas and stifle employee commitment.

Trust and Work Roles

Differing degrees of trust are implicitly expressed in the design of work roles. Jobs can be carefully prescribed or highly discretionary; they can be structured with narrow or diffuse responsibilities. Job specifications are either impoverished or enriched. Each approach has a different effect on trust.

Impoverished work rules are one of the features of highly bureaucratic environments. Specialization, the signature of bureaucratic work design, is efficient. Various specialized jobs make up the components of machine bureaucracy; integrating and harmonizing their workings ensure that the machine will run smoothly. Another advantage of job specialization is that it makes it easier to recruit, train, reward, and evaluate performance. Still, impoverished work roles (no matter what their practical value) do not make people feel they are trusted. They put people into boxes and reduce their scope of action.

Importantly, highly constrained work roles do not allow much room for new learning. When people come to work, only part of their job relates to the specifics they interviewed for; a significant portion of what they have to do is learn new things. One of the usual reasons employees are selected for a position is a combination of their actual skills and evidence of learning potential. More than one interviewee, for example, has secured a position by persuading the hiring authority that they were a fast learner. Organizations hire potential as much as anything else. It will not do them much good, however, unless they position themselves to capitalize on it.

High-discretion jobs trust people to use judgment about how to handle the uncertainty involved in all work. In low-discretion jobs, people are programmed to act in a certain way regardless of their reading of what a situation actually calls for. Narrowly specialized work arrangements, while perhaps suitable for mass production enterprises, are not appropriate for the kind of work most often performed in service organizations. These organizations call for allowing staff to have greater latitude because much of what is produced is a quality of human interaction or relationship rather than some kind of durable good.

Hidebound systems stifle participation and deny staff the ability to get involved in delivering quality service. The public employee, for instance, is most often guided by carefully detailed regulations about how to do work, but the real job of delivering public goods and services can be as much art as anything else. It is also very personal. Unlike the industrial worker, the public functionary often engages the "customer" in a face-to-face encounter, and the success of the event—its quality—depends upon the parties' interpretation of it. It is impossible to fully establish rules and procedures for all the contingencies and nuances of each individual confrontation. Yes, there are general rules that guide the behavior of the bureaucrat, but they can be based as much on internal standards as explicit rules.

In the final analysis, what public employees do in their jobs day to day is based upon "reflection in action," where they rely on an experience-based knowledge of what is actually happening—socially constructed reality—to guide their movements. The essence of this reality defies prior managerial calculation and control (Schoen, 1983). Employees must be permitted to retain a reasonable level of authenticity during these human engagements; they must be trusted to manage their own emotions and stay in touch with their real feelings.

Enlightened organizations must trust employees with sufficient time, space, and authority to make the necessary deductions about what a situation calls for, rather than force them to operate based on the illusion of the superiority of preprogrammed rules. A significant measure of hands-on judgment is called for to do any kind of work well. In many respects, all work is craftlike and requires a person to rely on feel, intuition, and judgment. Most people put their personal imprint on even the simplest work. The more they are trusted to do so, the better the product or the service (Carnevale and Hummel, 1993).

Benefits of Participation

The appeal of employee participation has deepened in recent years in both the public and private sectors. The importance of involving staff at work is a key idea embodied in Japanese management techniques (Ouchi, 1981) and prescriptions for achieving excellence in organizations (Peters and Waterman, 1982), a component in high-performing work cultures (Deal and Kennedy, 1982), and the most essential element in producing quality goods and services (Deming, 1986; Juran, 1988). Most recently, involving people is the cornerstone of the movements to reinvent and revitalize government (Osborne and Gaebler, 1992).

Despite recent enthusiasm, the advantages attributed to participation are not new. Earlier research investigated the effects of participation on leader and group effectiveness, the motivational needs of a changing workforce, productivity, job satisfaction, decision making and adjustment to change (Lewin, 1953; *Work in America*, 1973; Marrow, Barrows, and Seashore, 1967; Porter, Lawler, and Hackman, 1975). In fact, appreciation of the possible salutary effects of participation dates from the classic Hawthorne experiments (Roethlisberger and Dickson, 1939).

Several theoretical virtues are attributed to participation (Levine and Strauss, 1989; pp. 1900–1901):

1. Participation may improve decisions.
2. People tend to be more committed to the implementation of decisions they make themselves.
3. For some people, participation satisfies needs for creativity, affiliation, achievement, social approval and elevates their sense of power.
4. Participation improves communication and can increase identification with organizations if suggestions are adopted.
5. Participative workers learn to supervise themselves and develop leadership skills.

Most of all, participation augments people's experience and increases their learning. With all these benefits, why is it so hard to get organizations to permit people to be involved? The answer centers again on trust.

Earlier in my career, I spent a good deal of time trying to build high-performing labor organizations. These were institutions that could help people define their own interests and act in concert to realize their goals concerning work conditions. Most of my career was spent in going places that were in some kind of trouble: the membership was stagnant or declining; the organization was being raided; staff members were at each other's throats; the union had lost its political clout; there was a taxpayers' revolt; and so on. One of the first things I would do was to hire professional business agents to repair such problems. Missing from my equation was any belief that the membership of these organizations could save themselves. The model was high-energy visibility and advocacy on *my* part.

In one case, things were moving along as expected but not quite as fast as I wanted. So I engaged some consultants to help train organizers. I figured the consultants would come in for a weekend or two and energize the staff, and then we would hit second gear as an organization. They came in, conducted the seminars, asked a lot of questions, and then asked to meet with me. They wanted to know where the members were. I told them they were where they always were—out there somewhere, soon to be saved by the army of industrial social workers I was developing.

These consultants were Alinksy-style organizers; their sole interest was in building organizations from the bottom up. They had the radical idea that the members ought to learn to represent themselves. Rather than fixing their problems for them, they thought we should teach the membership how to mend their own difficulties. In the end, it would be a much stronger organization. They asked me why I did not involve the membership more. The answer was simple: because I thought they were all nice folks who knew very little about the requirements of representation. I just did not trust their ability to come up with the right strategies to confront very real, very serious issues. I was also afraid that, if I was not in control, all kinds of terrible things would happen.

Like what? the consultants asked. Well, I said, you could ask workers what to do with a bad supervisor and they might tell you to throw the person a party. I had actually heard that suggestion once. I thought that giving a mean supervisor a party was an absurd response and would obviously not be helpful, so I came up with something that I thought might work and that is what we did.

The consultants asked what was wrong with letting them throw the party for the supervisor. What was wrong, I replied, was that it could not possibly work; it might even make things worse. How did I know that? they asked. From my experience, I said; it was my experience that it could not work. Well, they offered, it was not within the experience of the *members* that it would not work, so why not let them try it? If the tactic failed, they argued, the members would try something else. They would be learning all the time and, eventually, they would find something that would be effective. In the process, the union would become stronger, more democratic, and effective. My strategy, they pointed out, was keeping the members dependent on me even when my methods were successful. When my techniques were not productive, they had me to blame. In either case, they never learned anything. Eventually, I would need to depend on them and could not because I had kept them small, limited their potential, and ignored what they knew.

The point took. I immediately internalized something about trust, real participation, and institution building that I have never forgotten. It was, by the way, wonderful to see an organization get "out of control." We were never better.

The idea of getting out of control is likely to be off-putting to many organizational leaders. After all, they have been socialized into believing that they must maintain control at all costs. The question is whether they are really ever in control or are just deluding themselves. Leaders are, in fact, largely helpless. To get done what is required in their organizations, they cannot act alone. They need to get everyone involved.

Forms of Participation and Problems of Trust

There are plenty of methods to encourage staff participation: Scanlon, Rucker, and Improshare plans, sociotechnical systems, job enrichment and redesign programs, assorted organizational development interventions, management by objectives, quality circles, and various quality of working life (QWL) initiatives (Lawler, 1986). Recently, implementation of total quality management

(TQM) in government continues the trend (Hyde, 1992; Swiss, 1992). While there are differences among these processes, they generally share the goal of increasing employee participation as a way to positively influence organizational achievement. There is strong evidence that it works.

The effects of participation upon individuals and organizational performance have received considerable notice. Participation generally encourages a sense of identification with the organization and a more positive quality of working life. Participation also results in higher productivity, decreased turnover, and increased job satisfaction.

All of this assumes, of course, that the participation is genuine. Participatory schemes promote trust only if they are credible. In other words, if the statement "we want you involved because we value your ideas" is experienced as empty rhetoric, employees will rightly become cynical. How many times have you been invited to participate in meetings where the outcome is already decided? How often are you invited to provide input only to have your ideas ignored? How often have you felt that you were included simply to legitimize a process where someone else's preferences were destined to prevail? Have you been left out of a meeting important to your job? Have you been given the silent treatment after you spoke up at a meeting? How do these pseudoparticipatory experiences influence your feelings of trust?

Real participation demands that people be able to communicate. The classic problem for organizations, arising from Taylorism, is the belief that if workers are allowed to think, they will do so with their own needs in mind. That is intolerable in some systems. For instance, a large computer company encouraged staff to use its electronic mail system to exchange ideas, and even tolerated its use for sharing personal information on hobbies, vacation tips, and the like. But when female engineers began to use the system to discuss their lower pay and inferior working conditions, the system was brought back under tight control (Richardson, 1992, p. 159). This is a case where management wants to gather and use the ideas of the workforce without giving up control over how the ideas will be used. In other words, the organization trusts people to think, but only to the extent they think about things management wants them to. Anything that might disrupt the social order is off limits.

Participation in Groups

Often, the most critical decisions in organizations are made by committees, teams, task forces, or other groups. A great deal of research shows that consensus decisions arising from groups with five or more participants are better than individual, majority vote, and leader decisions (Gibson, Ivancevich, and Donnelly, 1991). Despite these beneficial effects, however, there are problems with group decision making, arising from underlying problems of fear and trust.

Groups can sometimes make poor decisions because of intragroup dynamics where members lose their ability to think critically or refuse to express disagreement with dominant group perspectives. In the first case, excessive cohesiveness or group conformity drives out individual capacity for discriminating thinking. People's eagerness to trust in the group overrides their own analytical abilities. In the second case, people worry that others in the group will interpret their questioning as disloyal or threatening and ultimately they will be expelled from the group. Since group membership satisfies powerful individual needs, people are not eager to risk being punished for speaking out. This phenomenon is known as "groupthink"—the pursuit of group harmony and consensus overrides critical reasoning faculties (Janis, 1972). It cannot be overcome unless people trust that they can speak up and still be safe.

A military commander popularized an expression for encouraging participation and open communications in his unit: "Open Kimono." It means there is no shame in making mistakes, only in trying to hide them (Lusche, 1994). Wisely, this leader understands that bad news will not be brought forward if there is cost to the person reporting it. When there is retribution for speaking up in a group, there are no dividends of trust.

Groups will make mistakes when they try new things. Rather than punish them, wise leaders reward them. An office in the DuPont corporation thought it could increase productivity by installing a new computer system. The experiment failed, but rather than chastise those who suggested it, the company presented the group with a plaque that read: "We're proud of your effort and hope you try again as hard in years to come" (Dumaine, 1990). This non-blaming attitude builds trust.

Trust problems also surface between groups. Scarce resources, differences in goals, inaccurate perceptions, and disagreements about how to accomplish objectives can all lead to intergroup conflict and create significant conditions of mistrust. Systems depend upon the cooperation of interdependent groups and cannot function well for long if dysfunctional group conflict persists. There are numerous methods to resolve group dissension and most depend upon increasing levels of trust. For example, negotiating, compromising, mediating, team building, and other conflict resolution techniques depend heavily on trust. All these techniques aim to get people to communicate, to stop stereotyping each other, and to confront the consequences of their conflict for themselves and their organizations.

The bottom line is that being present in a room is not sufficient to qualify as truly participating. Authentic participation means having not just voice, but effective voice.

Unions Are Critical Groups

While an expanding body of research underscores the importance of employee participation systems, less consideration is given to the role of unions in such ventures. The issue of union involvement in decision making is unusually important in the public arena, where the extent of labor organization is roughly twice that of the private sector.

Labor and management have worked together since the early part of the century on all sorts of participatory programs. They have also cooperated on health and safety, wartime production, apprenticeship and training, employee assistance, energy and resource conservation, new technology, joint community fund drives, and other concerns (Cohen-Rosenthal and Burton, 1987).

Despite a history of alliance, some union leaders and managers remain mistrustful of participation and cooperation plans. The primary reason is that employee involvement policies hold different assumptions about the underlying nature of the employment relationship from traditional labor relations processes. Some union officials fear that participation programs undermine the local union, its officers, and collective bargaining. Unionists also know that participation programs, in all their forms, have been used in union-avoidance strategies. Behavioral science consultants, who have strongly supported employee involvement, have been seen as unfamiliar with unions and closely associated with management interests (Parker, 1985; Kochan, Katz, and McKersie, 1986).

The mistrust of union leaders toward participatory and cooperative programs is based on unhappy experience; in the past, such plans have exploited or ignored their interests. Kochan, Katz, and Mower (1984, p. 5) summarize this view: "Early proponents of QWL largely ignored the history of industrial relations and collective bargaining. . . . While industrial relations recognizes the need for *both* hard bargaining and mutual cooperation, the behavioral science theories upon which the QWL advocates derived their strategies ignored the conflict side of the employment relationship and stressed only the need for and value of cooperation. In their crudest form, the behavioral science theories were really theories *of management* developed *for managers* rather than theories of the employment relationship from which policies and practices could be derived for balancing the diversity and maximizing the commonality of interests at the workplace."

Managers have their own anxieties. They fret that collaboration is "soft," undercuts their authority, and threatens their livelihoods. Supervisors, for example, are jeopardized because the agenda of work teams can cut deeply into their jobs or eliminate them altogether (Hecksher, 1988). Middle managers, in particular, have been accused of subtly sabotaging more employee involvement efforts than any other group (Huszczo, 1991). Flattened hierarchies have accompanied many recent employee involvement efforts, and first-level supervisors and middle managers have seen their jobs threatened as a result. At bottom, employee participation and union cooperation procedures menace the ideology that it is the principal job of managers to command and control work operations and employee behavior.

The perceptions described above breed and institutionalize mistrust. However, unionization of public employees is extensive and cooperation between labor and management at every level is necessary before high performance is realized throughout the public sector. Continuation of an excessively adversarial labor relations model is a drag on organizational achievement. Overcoming barriers to cooperation is difficult, but not impossible (Carnevale, 1993).

Union-management partnership is possible. For example, the leadership of the U.S. Department of Labor and employees throughout more than 800 regional and field locations have established a joint Employee Involvement and Quality Improvement Project (EIQI) that has generated significant improvements in agency operations. In the Wage and Hour Division, for instance, there are more than 200 quality improvement teams working on more than 450 projects or issues, including delegating decision authority to lower levels, improving case management, strategic planning, and customer service. The Mine Safety and Health Administration has used EIQI to strengthen the mine inspection process. Offices of the Occupational Safety and Health Administration have used the program to modify complaint-handling procedures, streamline case file processes, and design new computer applications to improve services. A departmentwide program called Serving Our Customer has led to the creation of more than 750 work groups in 500 field offices; the groups have already generated thousands of improvement suggestions in agency operations. These instances show that management and labor can cooperate for mutual gain in the public sector (Armshaw, Carnevale, and Waltuck, 1993).

After a rocky start, the encouragement of more labor-management cooperation is now becoming a reality in the federal government. As part of the scheme to reinvent government, for instance, President Clinton ordered that labor-management partnerships be created throughout the executive branch. A National Partnership Council was formed to help encourage cooperative ventures. Interestingly, management was not included on the Partnership Council, which left managers in a state of shock (Hughes, 1994b). Bruce Moyer, executive director of the Federal Managers Association, said managers felt "chagrined" and "disenfranchised" by the form of the Partnership Council. He also worried that, without managerial representation, the council might come up with "lofty" ideas that had to be implemented by people who had no say in their development (Harris, 1993). Managers are now assured more input into the reinvention scheme, though they have had to fight hard for it.

What is interesting in this case is how the world was turned on its head by leaving managers out of the participation loop—a situation they had not experienced before and found most uncomfortable. They did not trust the decisions that would be made without their input. They resented the fact that their knowhow was being ignored. They were suspicious of an administration that felt it could improve government services without their ideas. What they got was a bottom-up view of how traditional bureaucratic organizations have always treated employees in the lower grades. They can now understand the consequences for trust building of not involving people in organizations.

A Trust-Based Warning About Quality and Reinvention Designs

All the issues about the public sector, trust, knowledge and participation converge in the redefinition of values currently being made as part of the quality and reinvention movements in public organizations. There is a great contemporary fanfare about total quality management and various "re-isms" in government. The question is whether employees can trust the promise of these latest participatory plans to improve the quality of their work lives.

It is widely held that both reform initiatives are forging a knowledge-based revolution at work. It is overdue. However, previous management innovations, all based on participatory premises, also claimed to radically reform the world of work. Each had its shining moment before falling out of vogue. Every time employees were promised, in some way, to be empowered. Will TQM and reinvention fundamentally change how work is done? Will meaningful participation truly be realized? Hopes are high, but no one is certain.

At a 1990 conference sponsored by the American Society of Public Administration (ASPA), every panel on quality improvement was packed. There was almost an evangelical fervor in the air. Some people were anxious to find out everything they could about how to implement a quality program. And many of those present spoke glowingly of success after success. (One has to wonder why, with so many quality experts in America, we have any quality problem at all.) But other attitudes were simmering. Federal employees in particular seemed to think they had seen all this before. And of course they had.

In the past few years, public employees have been virtually assaulted by varieties of participation programs. One woman told me that she felt employees were being "preyed upon" by change agents and management reformers. It is a good thing that continuous effort is being made to involve people at work, to permit them to have more control over their jobs, to redistribute authority, to move toward greater teamwork, and to encourage organizational learning. But as worthy as these objectives are (and as important as they are for trust formation), there is a point when unfulfilled promises dash expectations and take their toll on staff. There comes a time when people get weary of the latest personnel "program of the month." They may become cynical and mistrustful.

There remains a quick-fix mentality in organizations and in the political system. Many of participatory designs, no matter how promising, are not given sufficient time to work. Further, the public sector has a habit of swallowing whole every fashionable idea emanating from the private sector without regard for the unique and demanding operating domains of public organizations. For all the hoopla that invariably accompanies each innovation, the fact is that the world of work of most employees, public and private, has not gotten any better as a result of these ideas. When it comes to management innovation, there seems to be more going on in executive development seminars and academic journals than in real organizations.

Organizations are dangerously close to overselling what may well be very good, even innovative, participatory concepts. More-over, they are killing trust by their short attention span, by not giv-ing participatory programs a chance to work. When something that is supposed to be revolutionary really does not change the domi-nant management ideology, the net result is that organizations end up promoting cynicism. In spite of all the programs, the notion con-tinues, in most cases, that it is the manager's job to control the activities of the enterprise and to impose employee discipline. As a result, we may be fast approaching the point when it is rational for employees to be mistrustful of organizational improvement schemes, no matter what they claim.

The latest promise of systemic change in government is the reinvention effort at the federal level. It is too early to predict its future, but one observer warns: "Many companies have 'reinvented themselves' only to be hobbled later by a revolution of rising expec-tations. That's what happens when you tell people their ideas are wanted and promise them greater autonomy to make improve-ments, but then fail to deliver . . . employees soon will learn that managers talk big but don't listen, delegate work without the resources to do it and use tight budgets as an excuse for not deliv-ering. And hell hath no fury like a group of people whose expecta-tions were raised then frustrated" (Laurent, 1993b, p. 11).

In conclusion, the relationship between participation, trust, learning, and high performance is clear. Being allowed to partic-ipate in decisions at work influences people's sense of bureaucratic efficacy, helps them learn, positively affects their work performance, and increases organizational achievement. Participation centers upon the nature of work roles, which can be understood as expressions of trust. Therefore, designing jobs that show confidence in subordinates by allowing greater discretion is reciprocated by increased trust.

Participation must not be confused with pseudoparticipation. Superficial involvement and just plain fakery will destroy trust. People do appreciate the difference. Leaders cannot call for involvement in theory while pushing excessive conformity in practice. Meetings held to allow people to express themselves have to provide genuine opportunities for voice.

Public employees must be allowed greater opportunities to take part in decisions that affect them. Present work arrangements continue to be highly bureaucratized and out of balance with employee needs for involvement. The public sector plays an important role in society and its work practices must be state of the art.

More attention must be paid to the role of unions in participatory programs. It is an area given little more than lip service at the moment. Public organizations cannot be run as if unions do not exist. They do have something to contribute and need to be involved. Ignoring or attacking their legitimacy invites serious problems in achieving high performance.

Finally, the total quality movement and various "re-isms" represent the latest hope for institutionalizing participation and trust in public organizations, though the fate of their predecessors is not encouraging. Perhaps this time the drive toward empowering employees at all levels will endure. If not, trust will continue to erode.

6

Developing Effective Communications

Trust develops hand in hand with shared and truthful communication. And shared information is vital to performance. Trust depends upon the free flow of intelligence. This requires that people feel safe discussing their true thoughts and feelings appropriate to the work situation. They must also be able to disclose accurate, relevant, and complete data about problems without fear of negative consequences. Since innovation and creativity are important precursors of high performance, an environment must be encouraged where authorities are approachable, diverse ideas and opinions are welcomed, fear and reprisal are eliminated, critical thinking is encouraged, and disagreements are freely expressed.

Research suggests a strong relationship between levels of trust and openness in communication (Gibb, 1964; Schein, 1969). McGregor (1967), for instance, argues that trust in communications means that people can be themselves without fear of the consequences. When people feel safe from reprisal, they will reveal what they know or search for information they need to be true to the reality they face. It is often thought that open communications produces trust. Actually, trust and open communications go together. Trust encourages a person to use candor. When being open is not punished or confidences are not violated, the person is encouraged to continue to be open or even more frank. The cycle deepens and duplicates itself based on the self-heightening nature of trust relations.

The High Cost of Mistrust

Where open communications are suppressed, participants become suspicious and conditions for the free flow of information are short circuited—with devastating results. For instance: "A General Motors Corporation factory in Arizpe, Mexico, manufactured automobiles and engines. In May, 1986, managers discovered that the factory was producing defective piston casings. Their discovery triggered a costly recall of engines. What was 'very traumatic' for management was that some employees had known of the bad casings for as long as six weeks and continued producing the defective engines anyway. Employees said they feared that reporting the problem would land them in hot water" (Port, Carey, and others, 1991, p. 72).

Studies indicate that 70 percent of American workers are afraid to speak up with suggestions or to ask for clarification (Port, Carey, and others, 1991, p. 38). When employees' ideas are encouraged, however, good things can happen. For instance, a machinist at Tinker Air Force Base in Oklahoma felt that rejecting approximately 100 steel disks a day at a cost of $3,000 each was wasteful. He found a new way of dealing with the disk problem, which resulted in immediate savings of $700,000 (Fletcher, 1993). This kind of innovation is the result of a high-trust work climate where employees feel confident using their judgment, taking risks, and speaking up in the name of quality.

Genuine communication is the key to learning, for learning involves a dialogue during which people explore ideas, questions, and potential actions at all levels of the organization (Watkins and Marsick, 1993). It requires a climate of trust, feedback, and disclosure. It is a highly social activity and requires that people feel confident and safe. Fearful or suspicious people are learning disabled. They hide what they know and how they really feel. They are self-protective. They are reluctant to say what they mean. They camouflage their feelings to avoid perceived threat. Apprehensive people are not free to test their assumptions, to evaluate their actions, to reveal data, or to speculate about possibilities, if they think they are going to be embarrassed or punished. People learn very early in life to cover up if there is the chance that they will be humiliated or hurt.

If organizations value learning, they must encourage openness and trust. They must make the undiscussable discussable (Argyris, 1993). As Giffin and Barnes (1976, p. i) explain, "[in] order for effective communication to develop, *trust* is absolutely necessary. No matter what type of communication is being practiced, the foundation of the prescriptive literature advocates trust."

The Cycle of Trust-Based Communications in Work Groups

Zand's classic model of trust (1972) illustrates how trusting relationships rely on the interaction of communication, participation, and self-control in work groups. This model needs to be reinterpreted to highlight the relationship between trust, communication, and the creation of a shared knowledge base in work situations.

In the high-trust pattern, leaders initiate trust by being open about how they feel and what they are thinking. They do this knowing it increases their vulnerability to others whose behavior they cannot control. They risk sharing information with others and encourage them to use it in defining and finding solutions to problems.

They begin with an assumption of their interdependence with people in the group, and base everything they say on that assumption. They know it is the group that constitutes the reality of the work situation and therefore have faith that the group, whether openly or covertly, will participate in finding solutions to the issues at hand. This means that the leaders are relying on the self-control of the group members to regulate their own activities. All those involved, both leaders and followers, are accepting the mutual influence of one another on the knowledge base of the situation, grounded in a self-reinforcing cycle of trust.

Low-trust leaders, on the other hand, try to appear invulnerable. They do not share relevant information with the group. They use rules and regulations to control group activity rather than let the group decide what to do with a problem. Reality is distorted or denied. In the final analysis, mutual influence based on open communications does not materialize and low trust prevails.

As Zand (1972, pp. 237–238) explains: "Groups that develop high trust would solve problems more effectively than low trust groups, that is, they would do better in locating relevant information, in using their members' skills to generate alternatives, and in eliciting commitment. . . .[In low-trust groups] energy and creativity are diverted from finding comprehensive, realistic solutions, and members use the problem as an instrument to minimize their vulnerability. In contrast, in high-trust groups there is less socially generated uncertainty and problems are solved more effectively."

Friedlander (1970) finds the same forces at work in groups with a record of accomplishment. In his research, leader approachability, mutual influence, and the personal involvement and participation of group members are the keys to their success. These factors create defense-reductive climates based on trust rather than fear. The result is a better group performance.

The relationship of trust with enhanced group performance, finally, is summarized by Golembiewski and McKonkie (1975, p. 166), who believe that trust leads to:

More open exchanges of relevant ideas and feelings.

Greater clarification of goals and problems.

More extensive search for alternative courses of action.

Sharing influence more broadly among all participants.

Greater satisfaction among participants about their problem-solving efforts.

Greater motivation to implement decisions.

Greater feeling of interpersonal closeness or team cohesiveness.

Several of these points were brought home to me recently during a training session I conducted for executive nursing staff at a hospital facing serious problems. I was under the mistaken impression that I had been invited to a staff meeting to talk about the importance of customer service and quality; I figured that would take about an hour. A few days before I was to appear, I checked with the hospital's administrator to confirm my schedule. I was shocked to find out that they were expecting a half-day workshop. With all the composure I could muster, I gently asked what it was they believed I was going to do. They did not have a specific topic in mind; they just wanted some solutions to their situation. Here's our problem, the administrator in effect said; you take it from here.

Their predicament was that they were in a public hospital that had pretty much gone broke. As a result, they had to lay off a significant number of people. The local community did not want to lose the hospital and rallied in support. Some private money was found to keep the facility open. The hospital leaders had already determined that carving out a distinctive niche in the market was the key to their survival. The strategy was based on providing high-quality care to local families. Now the problem: this vision of quality service had to be internalized and operationalized by a staff that was demoralized, weary, and beaten down by recent events. It is the all-too-familiar case that so dominates the contemporary organizational landscape.

I showed up for the seminar (very early) with my bag of instruments, overheads, and a video or two on high-performing organizations. I was still unsure how to get started and what to do. So, after the introductions, I simply told the participants what I knew about their circumstance: they had almost gone out of business, a number of their friends had lost their jobs, they were working very hard to improve services, there was some trouble between two major staff groups, and, despite their best efforts, the patient count was not going up and they were losing a significant amount of money every month.

They all nodded in agreement as I recounted this unhappy tale. I then said I suspected that I had been hired to make them feel better about all that. They laughed. I quickly added I had this bag of stuff with me about leadership, motivation, intergroup conflict, and total quality management—all the usual organizational behavior games. I said that while I could probably keep them reasonably entertained, I was not able to fix this problem for them. I did, however, want to help as best I could, and I thought I could probably bring something useful to their discussions. I then asked them what they wanted to do.

The group atmosphere changed dramatically. I immediately felt part of them and they seemed at ease with me. Some barrier had been overcome. I think my honesty about my anxieties was considered open, humorous, and trustworthy. I had engaged in self-disclosure. They reciprocated in kind. We then worked together on these difficult problems, tried to get them in some sort of common perspective, and developed a measure of recognition that working together was the only way out of this mess.

This experience reinforces for me that candor and self-revelation are disarming, as long as they are not designed to harm anyone. Self-disclosure reduces fear. Although some people believe that it makes them vulnerable, I feel it does just the opposite: it makes a person formidable. When it is combined with a question—asking people what they want to do—it can be powerful. Self-disclosure is high trust. It says I have faith in you. Because people monitor initial encounters with great care, it is helpful to take off the mask, step outside the expected role, and join the group.

When you reveal unexpected and authentic information, channels of communication are opened up. If you are persistent with this uncovering, it drives the cynics crazy. But what about people who are really out to be harmful? Do the same thing. Even when someone forces you to fight, your response is much better when you do not have to carry fear-induced, excess weight around. People prefer straight talk to manipulation and having someone lay their cards on the table rather than create smokescreens. In the end, being direct is power.

Candor is a good place to start where people have already lost trust in how their situation is being grasped or depicted. This is true. But all work situations are fundamentally fragile. Certainly by the time we perceive a problem at work, the apparent solidity and density of a work situation should be questioned. It is very likely that unjustified trust—trust in an unrealistic picture of what is actually going on—is keeping the situation as it is: solid, stolid, dense, and resistant to change. Wherever high performance is the goal, recurrent revolutionizing of our picture of the situation is an ongoing requirement. This means having the courage to explode undue trust, show how trust is valid and valuable only where the truth is the goal, and start talking again trustfully about the problem of revealing this truth.

Interpersonal Styles and Trust

Communication is an attempt to reduce uncertainty or ambiguity in a situation through the exchange of information or knowledge. The simplest models of communication typically involve communicators who send messages through some medium to receivers who decode the data and provide feedback on whether the material has been received.

Much of the knowledge communicated in organizations flows between people in a face-to-face manner. There are a number of opportunities for distortion of messages in these encounters. Different frames of reference, selective listening, semantic problems, filtering, time pressures, poor listening skills, and communication overload are just a few of the many barriers to effective communications. In a general sense, they all subvert the credibility or trust people place in the messages directed at them. These are normal aspects of the background noise in organizational life. However, there are even more direct threats to trust.

One of the major obstacles to establishing trust in communications concerns the interpersonal style of communicators or the predispositions individuals have when they relate to others. Two important aspects of interpersonal style directly influencing trust and learning concern *exposure*, or the extent to which people reveal who they are, how they feel, what they want, and so on; and *feedback*, or the extent to which they are willing to listen to and process data from others about themselves (Luft, 1961). Trust is elevated by communicators who are open and aboveboard, feel free to expose what they know, and are prepared to obtain feedback. Taken together, high levels of exposure and feedback constitute openness, which consistently relates to higher trust and also makes learning possible.

A way of understanding how interpersonal communications styles relate to trust is demonstrated in Figure 6.1. The model shows how combinations of feedback and exposure either enable open communications and trust or obstruct communications and create mistrust. The higher the exposure and feedback arena, the more possible it is for sharing information, reaching understandings, and learning.

People with low exposure and low feedback develop a style of *masking*. "Masked" people are unable or unwilling to process feedback from others and, at the same time, reveal little about themselves. They are overdefended. Little gets through their carefully constructed facades and not much of their authentic selves is revealed. They tend to deal from the security of rules—theirs and the organization's. People like this are characteristically mechanical, detached, and bureaucratic. They are likely to be reacted to with some measure of distrust and hostility. After all, no one can be sure what designs exist behind the mask.

FIGURE 6.1. Interpersonal Styles and Trust.

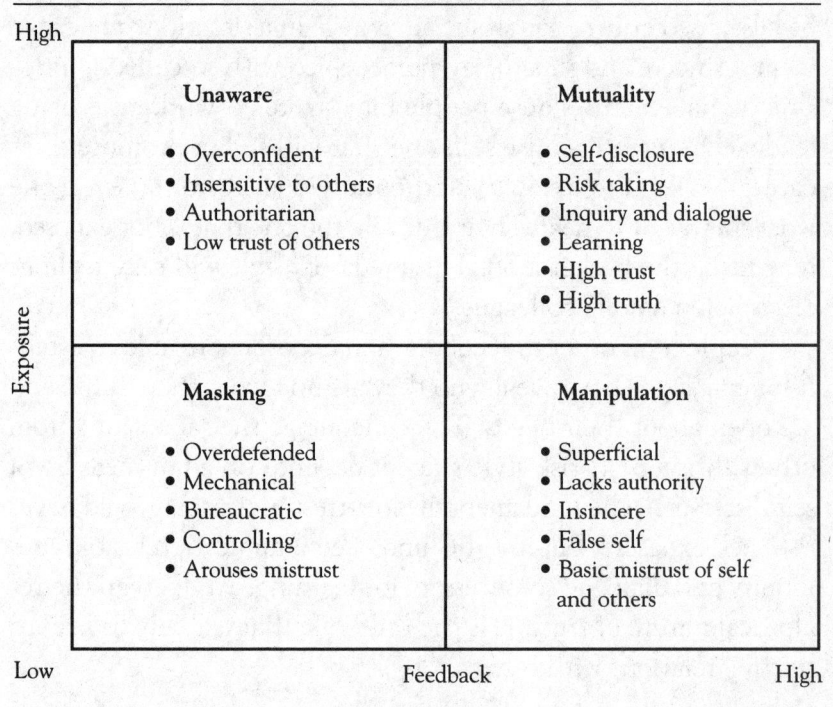

Adapted from J. Hall, "Communication Revisited," *California Management Review*, Spring 1973, *10*(3), 56–57.

People low on feedback and high on exposure are *unaware*. They do not process feedback from others and are not, as a friend once observed, ever disconfirmed: they hear the feedback but rarely internalize what it means. They are often too confident and authoritarian, which may well mask their distrust of both themselves and others. People in this group are learning disabled. They have limited their opportunities for growth by closing themselves off from the consequences of their behaviors and the benefits of fresh experience.

People high on feedback but low on exposure are seen as being in a stage of *manipulation*. They are busy taking in as much data as possible from their environment about themselves and others while revealing as little as possible about how they feel or what they believe. When they do reveal their feelings and attitudes they may be false, used only to gain some advantage in a situation. They may seem insincere and superficial, preoccupied with so-called impression management. These people may strike co-workers as using feedback to create a false self, one that will sell or promote their careers. These are likely to be the individuals who tell everyone what they want to hear. Their true self, the one that is not exposed, remains in the background. This predatory style will raise feelings of suspicion among colleagues.

People high on both feedback and exposure are able to establish *mutuality*. They reveal who they are and what they think, and are open about their needs. They encourage the same thing from others. It is a high-risk style since it depends on a fair measure of self-disclosure. The fundamentally low-trust individual would never risk such exposure. But it is the kind of communication that invites inquiry and dialogue so necessary for learning. And, given the reciprocal nature of trust, it is the one style that is likely to lead to trusting relations with others.

More Problems in Communicating

In addition to problems associated with self-presentation strategies, a second problem in establishing trustworthy communications concerns deliberate misrepresentation. One of the facts of life in organizations is that some people lie. Lying is consciously misrepresenting facts or omitting vital information in order to deceive another person. Lying destroys trust.

There is considerable deceit—or worse, perceptions of it—in public and organizational discourse. For example, when asked whether there is more or less honesty in government today than ten years ago, 75 percent of recently surveyed Americans report less (Gray, 1992). Moreover, a significant number of employees feel that the management of their organizations tells half-truths, puts a false face on things, trades in disinformation, and purposely obfuscates communications in an effort to exploit people (Kanter and Mirvis, 1989).

Tellingly, many people believe that a good rule of thumb in organizations is to mistrust anyone who uses what is called a "candor pander"—introducing a statement with something along the lines of "in all candor," "quite frankly," or "to tell the truth." As Shapiro (1992, p. 38) aptly observes, "Veracity these days is rare enough that its presence need not be advertised with self-congratulatory words."

A third problem in establishing trusting communications is that people communicate in more than words. Kinesics or body language is a communications medium. More feelings and intentions are probably communicated by facial expressions, eye contact, hand gestures, posture, and other forms of nonverbal contact than all verbal methods. When a sender's communication is contradictory, when the nonverbal message is at odds with the verbal message, the receiver places more weight on the nonverbal aspects of the transmission (Keltner, 1970).

Disparity between what is being said and what the receiver is actually observing raises suspicion. An inability to look someone in the eye, for example, is taken in the American culture as an indicator of distorting or suppressing information. Source credibility—whether a person is trustworthy—is a function of both what is and is not said in interpersonal communications.

Consistency in communications involves more than a match between words and body language. It requires a good fit between words and deeds. In the current vernacular, it means "walking the talk." A credibility or trust gap is instantly created when organizational authorities talk one way, then act another. Trust problems originate, for instance, when leaders call for joint sacrifice yet maintain their own perks. A credibility issue is also raised when agency heads bemoan the fact that the public unfairly bashes public employees, then are quick to blame their own agency personnel at the first sign of trouble. It is tough to trust people who elbow their way to be first on the lifeboat. Loyalty of the kind that builds trust and high-performing work communities is a two-way street. Trust is the first casualty when top officials do not make their deeds fit their words.

A fourth deterrent to trust is the chilling tendency of getting even with people who speak their minds. A "kill the messenger" mentality ruins trust. Knowledge cannot be shared in an atmosphere of anticipated reprisal for expressing ideas. An open communication climate exists when dialogue is encouraged on organizational issues, and tolerance of differing viewpoints is advocated. Employees feel comfortable speaking their minds only when they know it will not be held against them later on. Leaders who repress inquiry, genuineness, spontaneity, and open dialogue kill both learning and trust in their organizations.

An example of communication reprisal was brought to light in a recent report on the U.S. Forest Service. It was alleged that "Forest Service employees who speak out are discredited . . . crass intimidation occur[s] at virtually every national forest . . . [and] the Forest Service's reputation for 'muzzling' its employees is well-documented" (Walker, 1994, p. 2).

Striking back against employees who reveal agency wrongdoing is still a major problem in government. A recent survey of whistleblowers in the federal government, for example, gave the Office of Special Counsel (which is responsible for protecting whistleblowers) low marks for fairness, efficiency, competency, responsiveness, and communication. Eighty-eight percent of the whistleblowers surveyed said they had suffered reprisals and 47 percent said they had been threatened because they had tried to reveal wrongdoing. The bottom line was that the whistleblowers reported that they had paid a price for speaking out. Fully 93 percent felt that there was not enough protection against reprisal (Hughes, 1994a, p. 4). It is little wonder that some staff are reluctant to speak out against organizational misconduct.

One final difficulty: In organizations, there is often a willing, silent conspiracy to keep uncomfortable things off the table. Certain issues are avoided, bypassed, and covered up, never confronted directly. They lie just under the surface at meetings and people tiptoe around them with great care. Most employees can quickly jot down items that ought to be talked about but never get addressed in their organizations. That is because getting these landmines diffused is dangerous business. It is safer to discuss them outside formal channels, easier to repress them altogether.

These defensive, low-trust communications are a way of avoiding embarrassment and saving face (Argyris, 1993). And they are pathological. They interfere with group learning and organizational change. Organizations cannot keep information down. People need to talk about what bothers them.

In fact, people *do* talk about what bothers them. When organizations do not permit open dialogue, individuals find alternatives they can trust. They surface issues at the water fountain, in restrooms, in corridors, at lunch, or in after-hours spots. They go to the union. They call trusted associates at home after work. The grapevine begins to buzz and the rumor mill churns.

The grapevine is alive and well in all organizations and, as everyone knows, it carries fairly reliable information. People tend to depend upon the grapevine when they are anxious, insecure, or threatened; some observers believe workers get the majority of their on-the-job information from it (Half, 1987). Rumors are currently flying around the U.S. Postal Service and throughout the federal government, for example, as the reinventing-government agenda moves forward and more and more agencies face reductions in force.

Managers are often encouraged to plug into the rumor mill and monitor what is going on there. That is good advice, for two reasons. First, often the kinds of issues that are on the wire are precisely those items that organizations try to bury and cannot. Second, the grapevine is a clear tipoff on how well the formal systems are performing. If an organization is in the kind of shape where the only way to communicate about the things that really bother staff is off the board, then employees are saying they do not have much confidence in official communication methods or the folks who control them. But, as we have painfully learned, employees do get their unhappy messages across in the quality of their products and services. Products and services *talk!*

Learning and Open Communications

The enthusiasm for all the management philosophies of recent years is based on trying to connect with employee knowledge. But that is only part of the story. What must be secured and employed in high-performing organizations is *new* knowledge. Effectively capturing and capitalizing on this emerging wisdom depends absolutely on effective communication.

The principal communications issue in high-performing organizations is not simply to trust what people know or to make sure the entire volume of an organization's communication material is processed efficiently. It is whether the especially fresh intelligence, the capacity-expanding raw material of learning, is communicated and put to good use by the organization as a whole.

Organizations and their employees do not operate in static environments. What any particular individual understands about doing the work is not enduring or stable. There is no such thing as fixed knowhow, and organizations cannot depend upon the illusion that it exists. If it did, most organizations would eventually capture everything they need to know. The fact is that knowhow is always evolving. Knowledge is never available in a complete or fully predictable state, nor will it ever be.

Organizations, like plants, have to adjust to their environments to survive. Just as with plants, the sun is not always out in work organizations. Organizations also experience their own forms of rain, hail, snow, or drought. These events can be anticipated and planned for, to some degree, based on past experience. But no two occurrences are ever the same. Each trial presents its own set of fresh demands that require innovative thinking. Creativity is always needed to deal with the subtleties, slight variations, or nuances of situations that superficially appear to be, but are not, like others that have presented themselves before. Inventive learning is always required.

Findings are constantly being supplied by people who toil at organizational boundaries, have their hands on products and services, and spend their time talking about and making sense of what is going on around them. If what is being learned is not allowed to be shared, then the organization may be headed for trouble.

The Problem of Hierarchy

The design of organizations must allow information to flow in all directions: upward, downward, horizontally, and diagonally. Hierarchy is an essential feature of classic, low-trust bureaucratic layouts that dominate the organizational world. These blueprints have their virtues. However, a major liability of hierarchical arrangements is their inability to handle two-way information rapidly and accurately.

Organizations in the contemporary world need to be fast on their feet. They must capture intelligence, evaluate what it means, learn from it, and rapidly adjust work processes in response to the feedback that the operating environment provides. The fast transmission of appropriate and accurate data is prized in high-performing organizations. It is the raw material for learning and is consequential only if it is timely and reliable. Excessive hierarchy—and one of its usual offspring, the centralization of decision authority—impede the relaying of worthwhile information.

People at all levels in highly stratified organizations are well advised not to trust the information that is rolling around. This is because messages are routinely "stepped on"; that is, their content is altered as they move within bureaucratic structures. Hierarchical distortion is recognized as a persistent problem in bureaucratic organizations (Tullock, 1965; Downs, 1967). No matter which direction information flows, its content is condensed.

This compression of information is efficient, but in the process data are lost. Judgments, driven by the psychologies and motivations of various personality types, are made about what to take out and what to retain. For instance, people often throw out the bad news while accentuating the positive. There are powerful incentives in many organizations that encourage people to try to take credit for good news while evading responsibility for anything remotely negative. More to the point, communications are used to defend and grab power.

The usual prescriptions offered to improve the conduct of communication in bureaucratic organizations tend to reinforce the very structures that create the problems in the first place. For example:

1. Communication can be improved by establishing grievance procedures, monthly labor-management meetings, open-door policies, employee suggestion award programs, and ombudspersons.

2. Management by walking around, holding organizational versions of town meetings, establishing employee focus groups, and conducting periodic surveys are considered useful.

3. Detailing and formalizing ever more work rules is an additional option.

4. Decentralizing work activities is yet another.

The problem is that none of those antidotes changes the fundamental nature of the organization's design. Its central organizing idea still rests on trusting that upward and downward communication is needed in some appropriate distortion-proof volume. The belief in the inherent superiority of making important decisions higher up the organizational ladder endures. Relatively long chains of command are still maintained.

At heart, these remedies are not high trust. They continue top-down control and are mere efficiencies used to sustain the dominant system. They are the equivalent of cholesterol reducers in the human body: they clean out the passageways to ease information flow. Much more is required to improve communications and trust in organizations. To really enhance communications, the organizational architecture must be fundamentally altered. The very need for upward and downward communication about how to do the work must be reduced or eliminated altogether.

The communication dysfunctions endemic to hierarchy are significantly reduced when employees are trusted to make decisions based on their intimacy with the work process and direct, swift access to necessary information. The locus of decision making at the point of production and service invites a different kind of communications pattern than is found in classical hierarchies.

Teamwork, Open Communications, and Trust

High-performing organizations rely on teams rather than individuals to get the work done. A *team* is a kind of work group that "is an officially sanctioned collection of individuals who have been charged with completing a mission by an organization and who must depend upon one another for successful completion of that work" (Alderfer, 1987, p. 211). According to Buchholz and Roth (1987, p. 14), high-performing teams demonstrate the following attributes:

1. Participative leadership—creating an interdependency by empowering . . . others.
2. Shared responsibility—establishing an environment in which all team members feel as responsible as the manager for the performance of the work unit.
3. Aligned on purpose—having a sense of common purpose about why the team exists and the function it serves.
4. Creative talents—applying individual talents and creativity.
5. High communication—creating a climate of trust and open, honest communications.

Why teamwork hinges upon excellent communications is

explained by Cox (1993, p. 31): "Information is an important point of leverage for effective teams. Free access to information improves team performance for several reasons. It enhances self-management, coordination, and adjustment to changing conditions by making teams aware of task requirements, available resources, and standards for evaluation. Information can also motivate performance by providing feedback on how well teams are performing in relation to their goals."

Work teams handle a great many responsibilities formerly assigned to individuals at higher levels in hierarchies. Nearly all of these obligations involve communications. Setting goals, making assignments, scheduling, providing feedback about performance, and evaluating quality are primary group activities. To do these things, team members engage in a number of communications activities. Manz and Sims (1984, pp. 416–418), for example, find that coordinators of work teams must be able to exhibit the following communication and trust-related behaviors to make teams work well:

1. Tell people (teams and individuals) when they do something well.
2. Tell the truth even when it may be disagreeable and even painful.
3. Encourage team members to openly discuss problems.
4. Act as a communication link between a team and . . . support group[s].
5. Encourage mutual trust and respect.
6. Be an information resource.
7. Share all information possible.
8. Be a happy listener.

What is being said here reinforces the basic notion that for good communications openness, trust, and facilitative rather than directive behaviors are required. Clay Carr (1991) underscores this view when he explains that one of the most important roles in leading self-managed workers involves ensuring that information flows freely throughout an organization by creating and maintaining trust. He encourages listening actively and responding honestly to others' ideas, discussing all suggestions openly, making and keeping one's commitments, and having integrity as solid bases for building trust.

7

Fair Performance Appraisal and Incentive Systems

Fairness in the administration of rewards and disciplinary policies is a significant predictor of trust in organizations (Carnevale and Wechsler, 1992). Trust is elevated when people see that reward and punishment decisions are based on performance-related criteria. In addition, trust is strongly related to "process control"—that is, whether employees have some meaningful involvement in how such determinations are made.

It does an organization little good to build high-powered learning systems and then let them be subverted by feelings of inequity because the incentive system is mismanaged. People may have faith and confidence in themselves and their organizations because they have chances for voice and involvement on the job, but that is going to matter very little if they think their contributions are not being fairly recognized and compensated.

Employees are especially sensitive to fairness in order to protect themselves from being exploited (Gouldner, 1960; Ouchi, 1981). When people have confidence that the administration of an organization's inducements are impartial, they respond with trust. People who do not feel honorably treated mistrust their organizations. They also tend to be less productive and satisfied. They are absent and quit their jobs more often than their high trust counterparts (Oldham and others, 1986).

Increasing trust does not necessarily mean paying higher compensation but making sure that it is allocated equitably. Trust is gained not by avoiding discipline but ensuring a measure of fair play. Trust is elevated not by using a particular appraisal instrument but by giving staff an opportunity to have some part in the procedure. Trust is not a function of outcomes alone but the processes that are used to administer rewards and discipline.

Organizational Incentive Systems

An organization is an economy of incentives designed to recruit, retain, promote social equity among, and motivate employees. Organizations use them not just to get people to join up and stay aboard but to sustain their involvement, motivation, and commitment. These incentives are based on an organization's ability and willingness to pay. Incentives are both material (money, perks) and nonmaterial (status, prestige, and power). They can be tangible or intangible. They are both extrinsic (coming from others) and intrinsic, emanating from the nature of the work itself (Barnard, 1938; Simon, 1948; Lawler, 1971).

Incentives are designed to appeal to people's needs, drives, and goals. They are built on various motivation theories that seek to understand the specific needs within individuals that energize, focus, sustain, and stop behavior. Once these are comprehended, appropriate rewards are offered to optimize performance. No two people's needs are quite the same. They vary by experience, the importance of work as a central life activity, and cultural and demographic factors. People are complex, and a wide range of inducements must be used to motivate them over time.

The mix of motivators for public employees reveals a somewhat different blend than those found for private personnel. There is evidence that government employees place less value, for instance, on pay, although this indication varies by organizational level, geographic area, occupation, and type of agency. Uniquely, government employees also place a high value on work that allows them to engage in "meaningful public service," or helping others and society, while satisfying their own needs.

Public service motivation is driven by a number of different desires. Some are purely rational, others are more altruistic. In any case, one thing is clear: allowing public employees to realize their motivation toward service, whatever its bases, enhances commitment to their organizations (Rainey, 1991, pp. 129–133; Perry and Wise, 1990). Frustrating these needs invites negative attitudes. A study of state employees in Florida, for instance, shows that frustration of a generalized service ethic interferes with trust formation (Carnevale and Wechsler, 1992).

The exact combination of motives may vary between public and private staff, but the basic tenets of motivational theories hold. In principle, organizations must provide ample resources to reinforce people's basic and higher-order drives. They must supply acceptable pay, competitive benefits, decent working conditions, and chances to control their jobs. The range of inducements should be broad enough to appeal to the extent of needs exhibited by the typically diverse workforce. Employees will demonstrate expanded trust in organizations that try to improve the quality of their work lives in these ways.

When it comes to issues of trust, the question for organizations is not whether they have provided enough incentives for all their workers, but whether those rewards are administered fairly. Fairness is embedded in two popular and empirically supported motivation theories: expectancy and equity theory.

Expectancy theory centers on perceptions of the likely relationships among effort, performance, and reward. For instance, when people see something they value (valence), they determine what they have to do to get it (instrumentality). This association is known as a performance-reward expectancy. If they have confidence in their ability to do the thing it takes to get the reward (expectancy), a positive force is created and they will be motivated to try to realize their objectives (Vroom, 1964).

Expectancy theory brings to light how both content and process issues interact to influence attitudes of fairness and trust in the administration of rewards. When a potential reward is sufficiently motivational, people will try to figure out what is required to get it. Suppose the valence is a promotion or bonus (or both) and the instrumentality (what it takes to get these rewards) is the successful completion of a particular project. Employees are led to believe that effective management of the task leads to the prize. Trust is now on the table. If employees do what was expected and the promised bonus is given, trust is reinforced. If the bonus does not materialize, the performance-reward linkage is disconnected and trust is shattered.

Employees become understandably cynical when anticipated payments do not follow accomplishment. Of course, there are always the hopeful among us, much like Charlie Brown trusting that Lucy will not take away the football just as he attempts to kick it. The reward for poor Charlie's faith is always the same: each season he ends up on his back. After a while, even the most optimistic people learn not to get suckered. Their trust is used up.

Equity theory is another process concept that bears on trust. Equity theory suggests that employees seek a satisfactory return on their investments at work. They compare themselves to others to determine if they are being equitably rewarded (Adams, 1963, 1965). Employees have a good deal of lateral vision. They are always measuring how they are faring compared to others. In organizations, people make investments (time, effort, commitment, identification) in exchange for pay, promotion, recognition, and the like. People expect a just return on these investments, the receipt of a fair share of benefits roughly proportional to costs. According to Homans (1961), if fairness is not forthcoming, people will react negatively. One negative repercussion is that employees will lose faith, confidence, and trust.

In summary, the message in the administration of incentives is clear. First, rewards must be available in sufficient quantity and quality to satisfy people's needs at work. Second, expectancy theory shows that what is promised must be delivered or trust will suffer. Third, equity theory teaches that, while the absolute amount of rewards certainly does matter, how they are relatively allocated is most crucial. Equity theory also instructs that, whether you are cutting a small cake or a large one, the size of the portions are monitored closely. Even a large piece is not satisfactory, if someone feels someone else's slice was bigger than it should have been.

Contingent-Pay Systems

Government workers like the idea of pay-for-performance systems but often do not trust the ways they are administered. These systems are beset by a host of problems that conspire to subvert trust and create enormous unrest among staff:

1. There have been consistent problems in allocating enough money to support such plans.

2. Some employees suffer a loss of esteem and are demotivated if they do not receive benefits under the system (Meyer, 1975).

3. People are labeled winners and losers as a result of these plans. Deci (1975) argues that contingent-pay systems undercut intrinsic motivation because people concentrate only on what gets extrinsically rewarded and ignore other important, but not compensable, behaviors.

4. These are really *individual* merit-pay programs, and thus teamwork may suffer (Deming, 1986). A kind of destructive individualism is promoted as people compete for scarce opportunities. In some organizations it disintegrates into a zero-sum process, a war of all against all.

5. Employees do not often get a chance to participate in system design and administration. It is usually someone else's procedure, not theirs, that is being used.

What does not get enough attention in studies of contingent-pay programs is the low-trust assumptions that caused them to be introduced in the first place. There is a popular misconception that setting up one of these plans represents a sincere attempt at positive reforms in personnel practices in the name of producing better government. Frequently, the truth is something else altogether.

There is a habitually low-trust, negative bent to the premises underlying the creation and diffusion of so-called merit-pay systems. Too often, these plans are introduced on the heels of criticism of bureaucratic performance. They are intended to be bitter medicine to get people producing or managers managing. They are regularly premised on negative stereotypes of public employees.

To make matters worse, they are quick-fix strategies not customarily integrated with other necessary system changes—especially those that cost money. Comprehensive change strategies aimed at improving bureaucratic performance are costly. They involve some degree of new investment to work well. Merit-pay programs do not require such investment. They are meant to lower costs and increase control. And that is not all: These programs are typically introduced to put a happy face on a bleak fiscal reality. When there is not much money around, elected officials can spend less on raises and still pick up some political capital by adopting such strategies. It is good government at half the price. It is also a way to take the high road when a legislative body does not have the political courage to pay an entire workforce a cost-of-living raise. Finally, much of what drives the diffusion of pay-for-performance prescriptions is based on the largely untested and incorrect assumption that it is working well in the business community and, therefore, ought to be swallowed whole by the public sector (Ingraham, 1993).

Employees are not opposed, in principle, to such designs. Quite the contrary. In a recent survey of federal workers, 72 percent agreed conceptually that some portion of their salaries should be tied directly to performance (U.S. Merit Systems Protection Board, 1990). The difficulty is that they, like government employees at all levels, are skeptical of these techniques because they live in a world of mean-spirited bureaucrat bashing, blatant political opportunism, and broken promises when it comes to compensation in general and contingent-pay plans in particular.

Of all the problems encountered around the administration of incentive systems, none is more powerful than the common mistrust of appraisal methods used to draw conclusions about who gets a raise. There is also an associated, significant suspicion about the credibility of supervisors who administer these programs. If employees do not believe that appraisal operations are fair, they will not trust any pay-for-performance design (Lawler, 1981).

The Lack of Confidence in Performance Appraisal

Perhaps no personnel technique has received more attention than performance appraisal. It is a process that has great intuitive appeal. Politicians think that employee evaluations ensure high performance. Managers think that it enhances their control. The more human relations–minded are encouraged to feel it enables them to coach subordinates and "facilitate" better performance. Personnel specialists tolerate the process because it gives them documentation for various change-of-status actions that is useful in an increasingly litigious operating context. Employees accept these methods because they crave feedback on their performance and believe that the best among them should be rewarded for superior effort. Finally, appraisal reinforces deeply held values fundamental to the American character where getting, holding, and advancing at work is thought to be based on individual achievement. The problem, of course, is that evaluation works a lot better in theory than in practice.

The difficulties with appraisal technology fall into two main categories: the failure to come up with reliable instruments, and the presence of various forms of rater bias.

There are many, many kinds of appraisal methods, including graphic rating scales, narrative essays, weighted checklists, forced-choice ratings, peer reviews, subordinate evaluations, paired employee comparisons, self-rankings, critical incident techniques, and behaviorally anchored ranking scales. Each has its own set of advantages and drawbacks when it comes to cost, reliability, validity, and acceptance among users (Dresang, 1991; Moore, 1985; Hays and Reeves, 1984). Detailing the relative strengths and weaknesses of each is less important than recognizing that none enjoys high levels of faith and confidence by organizations that use it or employees who are subject to it.

In addition, all these appraisal methods share some common rater problems: the halo and horns effects, personal bias, leniency/strictness errors, central tendency, special group feeling, lack of rater training, spatial and psychological distance, and recency influences (Lovrich, 1990). Central tendency error means that an evaluator tends to rate all subordinates as average no matter how they actually work. This occurs when evaluators fear the repercussions of making difficult judgments about the real contributions of employees. Special group feeling error means that an evaluator is captured by a group's cozy feeling and is therefore unable to draw accurate distinctions about the contributions of individual group members. Recency error means that evaluators give too much weight to recent events. Therefore a person who has an outstanding success just prior to an evaluation is likely to be overrated, while a person who makes a significant mistake near evaluation time is overpenalized. These are all ways that perceptions of fairness are destroyed. In every case, employees have reason to believe that the deck is stacked against them. Appraisal is, in the final analysis, an imperfect human process and not an exact science (Nalbandian, 1981).

Taken together, instrument and rater deficiencies conspire to erode employee trust in the fairness of the procedures used to assess their performance. For example, in the U.S. Office of Personnel Management's 1979 federal employee survey, only about half of the respondents believed that their evaluations were fair. In a 1987

Merit Systems Protection Board (MSPB) study, fully 53 percent felt that there was an arbitrary limit on the number of people who could receive high ratings. A significant minority (36 percent) felt that supervisors gave identical ratings to people regardless of the quality of their work. Even more important, only one in four reported that they felt fairly treated with respect to awards decisions during the previous two years (U.S. Merit Systems Protection, 1987). In a 1990 MSPB report, even though ratings of staff were generally higher, a significant number still believed they were not fairly ranked, and only 42 percent would choose to be under a pay-for-performance system that relied on their supervisor's judgment of their job accomplishment. At the state and local government level, these methods are at least as dismal and probably worse (Shafritz, Riccucci, Rosenbloom, and Hyde, 1992; Ingraham, 1993).

One way to improve performance appraisal is to get rid of it. At McClellan Air Force Base in California, for example, an experiment called Pacer Share was put in place and individual appraisals were eliminated. According to one manager, "Nobody missed it, no one lost anything from it, and no one wanted it back" (Rivenbark, 1993, p. 12). In a somewhat radical recommendation, Bowman (1994) suggests that using traditional performance appraisal to assess and change individual behavior is misguided when work systems themselves are usually what is at the heart of poor performance, not individual failure.

Assuming appraisal methods will endure in organizations, working on forms of instrumentation and training people to conduct assessments in ways that minimize common biases will certainly help. However, real progress lies not in any technique but how it is used. Appraisals could be done on the back of envelopes and be better accepted, if employees felt they had some voice in the procedure and were assured a measure of procedural due process. Trust in appraisal techniques will be measurably elevated when employees have substantial involvement in how these mechanisms are designed and operated.

Procedural Justice and Trust

What makes an employee think a reward decision is fair? The answer that receives the lion's share of attention in organizational research is the concept known as *distributive justice*. This approach, derived from equity theory, "proposes that a 'fair' distribution is one in which there is an equal balance between the ratio of one person's inputs to outcomes and the input-outcome balance of another person" (Bies, 1987, p. 292). In other words, people evaluate whether what they get is equitable based on how much they contribute compared to others. This perspective concentrates on the *outcomes* of disbursement decisions. It is about content and consequences (Walker, Lind, and Thibaut, 1979).

An emerging area of personnel research takes a somewhat different tack in explaining how people assess the justice of reward decisions. In this approach, the fairness of organizational outcomes is explained, in large part, by *how* distributive decisions are made. This is the *procedural justice* perspective (Thibaut and Walker, 1975). The central argument is that employees will be more satisfied with outcomes if they trust the procedures used to make the determinations in the first place. This means that how decisions are made becomes paramount. If people do not trust the methods, they cannot have faith in the results (Folger and Greenberg, 1985).

Recently, several of my colleagues became frustrated with what they perceive as unfair pay practices for the extra teaching they routinely perform. There has been no adjustment in the amount of money they receive for their overload work in over a decade. They feel exploited and want something done about it. Since I have some administrative responsibilities with respect to the program that is the cause of their distress, they directed me to undertake negotiations on their behalf with the appropriate administrative authorities to get the matter settled.

The people who have the power to adjust their salaries have agreed to form a committee to study the issue and make recommendations for settlement. However, initially, it was not certain that any member of my department would be able to serve on that committee. Upon learning this, we immediately contacted the person putting the group together and advised him that the credibility of the study team was suspect. It would have little or no legitimacy with the people in the department if they were not directly represented at the table. My associates were suspicious already and a lack of any process involvement would lead to escalating mistrust and inevitable conflict down the road, no matter what the outcome of the procedure.

We now have a seat on the committee. In this case, as in so many others in the daily administration of organizations, how things are done counts every bit as much as what is done when it comes to trust.

In another case, I faced the task of negotiating a labor agreement on behalf of more than 100,000 state workers in a situation where the local union leadership throughout the state distrusted the national union. They felt they had been sold out in the past and had little faith that it would not happen again. My job was to get the best agreement possible but, more important, to repair the mistrust between the state council and the international organization. It was improving the relationship between various levels of the institution that counted. The contract was the means to that end.

In the past, contracts had been bargained by a professional staff person using a small committee of a dozen or so carefully selected union members, chosen mostly on the basis that they would not cause any trouble and ratify the results of the negotiations. Since the problem was one of trust, I decided to try something different. No matter what the outcomes of the negotiations might be, the local unions had to participate in the process.

We appointed a bargaining team of over sixty local union presidents who attended every session, took turns at the table, spoke for themselves on issues that mattered to them, caucused with staff before and after every session to evaluate strategy and results, and were very much involved from start to finish. From an outcomes perspective, this agreement was not particularly noteworthy. However, from a process point of view, the real agenda of improving the level of trust between the national and state union was something of a success. The members enjoyed a strong measure of process control and procedural fairness, which elevated satisfaction with outcomes and trust.

What people are looking for in both of these illustrations is effective voice-giving procedures. People want real input. Constructive input in evaluation decisions is not common in organizations. Or, to be more exact, dialogue is allowed as long as it does not rise to real dissent. How many times are performance appraisals done on the basis of only a cursory interview? And if there is an interview, how genuine is it? How often do supervisors fill out evaluation forms and instruct people to look them over, sign them, and, if they have no real problem with the results, return them for processing. If there is a conference between supervisor and employee, how frequently are supervisors willing to modify their decisions because of the employee's input? How many organizations have an appeals procedure available to staff who seek redress against unwarranted decisions? How many employees would trust using it, if one were available?

Employees will not trust conclusions made under circumstances where they have no participation, where all the ground rules are established by others, where there are no safeguards against abuse of authority, where bad decisions are not correctable, and where the legitimate concerns of all the parties are not fully represented (Leventhal, 1980; Leventhal, Karuza, and Fry, 1980).

When people feel wronged, they become morally outraged. At a minimum, they will stop trusting the purveyors of their injury. Disciplinary rulings, like reward determinations, have the same potential for causing anger and lowering trust in organizations. This is because they also rely on the identical shaky foundations of performance ratings and the extent of "fair process effects" in organizations (Greenberg and Folger, 1983).

Discipline, Due Process, and Trust

Disciplinary issues are unavoidable. Attendance problems, performance failures, misconduct, and dishonesty are legitimate reasons to take actions against employees. But, as everyone knows, these are not the only rationales. Abuse of power, vindictiveness, sexual harassment, personality conflicts, and plain lousy management are also explanations for why disciplinary procedures are used in organizations.

Whatever their motivation, disciplinary proceedings raise disputes and engender conflict. The question is not whether organizations will have such strife, but what kind of controversy they will have. Those that use high-input, high-trust procedures will fare better than those that do not. Trust is involved because people gauge the extent to which fairness is present in disciplinary proceedings, whether or not they are personally subject to them. At heart, trust reflects a judgment about whether people feel they have to protect themselves from harm. Of all work procedures, the conditions under which people are punished is probably the most significant tipoff to how much trust is warranted in an organization.

Disciplinary actions are hardly ever private affairs. Everyone, it seems, is watching how the organization handles these events, for it says a lot about the content of an organization's character. People know that what can happen to others might someday happen to them, and how their colleagues are treated says much about how much trust ought to be placed in organizational authorities.

What criteria do people use to judge fairness? In sum, whatever reflects their sense of fair play. Fair play depends upon several process-related questions:

1. Was there some forewarning that a particular type of behavior could lead to punishment?

2. Before deciding on taking action, did the employer investigate the charges against the employee? This does not obligate an employer to a full-blown inquiry. It does, however, mean

that the employees ought to have the chance to tell their side of the story.

3. Is the evidence against the employee substantial and compelling? Would a reasonable person, looking at the same set of facts, agree that some action was required?

4. Is there evenhanded application of the rules across employees over time? In other words, is the employer being consistent? In a recent local case, two women received a one-day suspension for fighting on the job. In this organization, males occasionally would skirmish too, but would not be sent home if they would shake hands and promise not to do it again. The women received such disparate treatment because management harbored the sexist belief that it was somehow more unseemly for women to come to blows. Of course the employer lost the case on appeal. Consistency in the application of rules counts.

5. Are the type and degree of discipline reasonably related to both the offense and the past record of the employee?

A "no" answer to any one of those five questions is likely to raise some issues of fairness among staff and lead to mistrust of the discipline system and the authorities who manage it. They are, in sum, indicators of due process.

Punishment is not an individual but a social affair. Disciplinary actions influence the behavior of observers in both direct and indirect ways. According to Trevino (1992), employees will judge an employer's decision not to punish a person for misconduct as unfair. When the punishment is perceived as fair, observers' reactions will be positive. However, when the decision to punish is seen as unfair, employee reactions will be negative, especially among those who closely identify with the disciplined employee or who are most committed to the organization.

Disputes about discipline in public organizations are likely to take the form of grievances, particularly since the public sector is heavily unionized. A grievance is an employee or union complaint about whether a punishment decision was based on "just cause" or good and sufficient reason. Like evaluations and pay decisions, how grievances are resolved is an important measure of outcome satisfaction. A decision in an employee's favor is not all that counts; how that decision is arrived at is also important.

Alternative Dispute Resolution

Traditionally, employee disputes have been settled through formal grievance procedures that resemble adversary arbitration. Usually outside third parties hear the merits of a dispute and impose final and binding decisions on the claimants. The arbitrator has significant control over both processes and decisions.

Recently, a collaborative dispute mechanism known as alternative dispute resolution (ADR) is being used more often to settle grievances (American Arbitration Association, 1987; Goldberg, 1989). Among its several advantages, one of the most important is that it allows disputants greater process control, which leads to more satisfaction with outcomes and higher levels of trust.

After the 1986 shootings in Edmond, Oklahoma, in which a postal employee killed fourteen co-workers, the Oklahoma City Division of the U.S. Postal Service introduced an ADR initiative called Union-Management Pairs (UMP). It relies on two-person teams composed of one union and one management representative. Team partners employ a highly participatory approach to settle disputes at the lowest possible level, using cooperation as the key. When the program was introduced in 1986, there were approximately thirteen hundred grievances pending in the Oklahoma City area. At the close of 1991, there were four.

What makes UMP work? First, participants get direct control over both processes and outcomes. People who have to live with the decisions are immediately involved in their settlement. The process is brought closer to the participants. It belongs to them.

Second, UMP promotes more face-to-face communication. In

the negotiating or confrontational model that is typical of traditional grievance procedures, communicating is like playing poker; participants understand that information confers advantage and they are not likely to share it. In the UMP program, a consensus paradigm is employed where all data are on the table. The team jointly investigates every complaint and makes its own recommendation for resolution. There are pressures on the teams to produce all the relevant facts.

Third, the UMP process is just plain faster. Research shows that employees will find a grievance procedure unfair if it takes a long time to get a decision, even if it is in their favor (Usery, 1972). The UMP process is, according to one participant, "quick." When asked how to improve the plan, he responded, "Quicker."

Fourth, increased trust is possible as the parties have experience working with one another over time. A substantial barrier to trust in dispute resolution is that the parties get so caught up in an escalating spiral of conflict that they simply go past the point of any chance of understanding each other's legitimate needs—a precondition to settling feuds. What transpires is not a problem-solving exercise but a war. The UMP program is just one example of how alternative dispute resolution can avoid these dynamics and build trust. And the process need not be limited to grievance disputes; it can be used effectively in marital controversy, environmental confrontations, and other forms of strife (D. G. Carnevale, 1993).

Some Final Thoughts About Incentives and Trust

The administration of rewards and punishments is a strong influence on levels of trust in organizations. Long before they ever show up at work, people have a powerful sense of what is fair in life. In all aspects of their existence, they measure the equities involved in their relationships and obligations. Individuals are more or less willing to allow transactions to ebb and flow in terms of self-interest and advantage. Most people, however, have a point where their willingness to continue to invest in affiliations will cease if they sense they are being exploited or their contributions are not being fairly recognized. At that instant, trust suffers.

Reward transactions are not the only kinds that bear on trust. Trust is very much about taking a risk in a situation where faith can lead to harm. Not getting a fair share of rewards is injurious, but it is not the same as getting harassed, suspended, or fired. It is not the same as having your life ruined. That is why people also pay such close attention to disciplinary events in organizations. Not being able to participate in decision processes is disappointing for many persons. Not being allowed to speak your mind is frustrating. Not receiving a well-deserved promotion invites anger. But being punished unfairly causes much deeper moral outrage.

The key to building trust when it comes to the administration of organizational incentives depends upon affording employees a fair measure of process control, effective voice, or procedural due process. People show increased faith in systems they help design and operate. Their satisfaction is enhanced when they have the opportunity to influence the means used to acquire outcomes. Feelings of justice and trust are strongly related to high-input processes at work.

8

Managing Power, Politics, and Conflict

Workplaces are not, as everyone knows, particularly well-ordered locales with common purpose, widespread agreement on what to do and how to do it, selfless activity, and sufficient resources. Scratch the surface of any organization and you will find something along the lines of a battlefield where people contest one another and jockey for survival. More than a few people head off to work every day prepared to do battle.

Power, politics, and conflict are interrelated, inevitable facts of life in organizations. These truths are not inherently good or bad. They represent the natural state of affairs and are part of the every-day drama of organizational life. Power, politics, and conflict are critical elements in the trust, learning, and high-performing organization relationship. When they are managed ethically or morally, they can build and sustain trust relations at work. When they are handled in an unethical or immoral way, they destroy trust.

Today the nature of work, and the problems of organizing and managing it, are radically changed. A wrench must fit the bolt. The tools in our traditional toolbox of power, to begin with, must fit the requirements of the emerging world of work. Some of our instruments must be recalibrated. Others must be thrown away.

For a long time, power has been based on mere position in hierarchy: "You must do it my way because I am above you and therefore superior to you." But now collaboration between technical fields is crucial to a system's functioning. Position power must yield to knowledge power. High performance lies in the profound difference between an order—"do it my way"—and a question: "What do you think we ought to do in this situation?" The knowledgeable at all levels of the organization must be able to trust that their knowhow will be supported. Position power or legitimate authority based on status alone must retreat in the face of the superior knowledge of all those throughout the organization who can construct the truth of a work situation based on their experience with it.

The prevailing concept of politics is borrowed from pluralist societies where people pursue diverse interests. There the public interest is merely the sum of all individual or group interests (Roelofs, 1992). However, the high-performing organization, even with all its divisions of knowledge specialists, is ultimately a unified enterprise. Everyone is in the same boat, rowing, intensely, in the same direction to accomplish some goal.

Organizations can continue to pursue the zero-sum politics of yore, in which what I win you lose, but if they do, achievement will be impaired. Americans especially—with our ideas of competing individually and in groups, often ruthlessly, for position, resources, and dominance—must acquiesce to nonzero-sum politics in which all gain in pursuit of a common vision. That approach is a tool that fits because the rule of the high-performing organization is precisely that the sum is greater than its parts.

This is not to say that conflict should be stamped out. It has its dark side when pursued in deadly serious games of wholly self-interested politics. But conflict can also shed light. In the equation of trust, the manager who is responsible for seeing to it that conflict is not allowed to get personal focuses on knowledge issues. In this respect disagreement and opposition, as well as other forms of conflict, can uncover the truth of a situation that false harmony often conceals.

Power, politics, and conflict can conceal the truth at work or bring necessary information to light. Where these dynamics facilitate dialogue and inquiry, trust and learning occur. Where they engender fear, low-trust, defensive conduct is the norm and learning is impaired. The trick is to manage the inevitable, conflicting human forces of organizations in a way that holds things together rather than tears them apart.

Power

As everyone who has ever worked in an organization knows, the nature of stratagems employed to deal with power, politics, and conflict inescapably leverage feelings of trust. Organizations are not unitary systems. They are pluralist societies where members pursue diverse interests. In the maneuvering that goes on, employees choose between ethical or indecent tactics to realize their goals. Organizations play their part as well. They establish the institutional framework within which these actions occur. They foster cultures that delineate the kinds of behaviors that will be tolerated. At all levels, these range from the civilized to the savage.

Power is customarily defined as getting people to do what one wants, despite their resistance. The classic explanation is Dahl's: "A has power over B to the extent that he can get B to do something B would not otherwise do" (1957, pp. 202–203). Power has also come to signify having the ability to "win" political battles and outmaneuver the opposition (Luthans, 1992, p. 426). Here, power is defined as a social force or "the ability to marshal the human, informational, and material resources to get something done" (McCall, 1978, p. 5). Using this meaning, power also indicates the ability to mobilize people to *willingly* work hard for organizational purposes. There are people who are extremely powerful in organizations because they have banked enormous amounts of good will that they can call upon when necessary to achieve their goals. They are both more formidable and more trusted than those who have to rely on force alone to achieve their ends. They are formidable because they are trusted. However it is defined, the main point is that any use of power that injures social relations impairs one's credibility and is not trustworthy.

Traditionally, the issue of power has been largely sidestepped by theorists who ignore its existence or underestimate its importance in organizational life. It has been more comforting, though inaccurate, to picture organizations as bland, cooperative systems that are meant to operate like clockworks. In this view, "everyone knows what the organization is all about and is concerned solely with carrying out its mission; people are basically happy at their work; the level of anxiety is low; people interact with each other in frictionless, mutually supportive cooperation; and if there are any managerial problems at all, these are basically technical problems, easily solved by someone who has the proper skills and knows the correct techniques of management" (Schwartz, 1990, p. 7).

From this perspective, disputes are seen as occasional ugly aberrations needing fast correction. They are viewed as exceptions to the rule of natural good order and harmonious relations: clockworks. The truth is that organizations are more like snakepits where self-interest combats self-interest and a good measure of stress and anxiety prevail (Schwartz, 1990).

Images of "power" should not, however, conjure up just negative impressions. Power is a necessary vitality and strategic contingency for getting things done in organizations. As one writer unapologetically observes, "It is powerlessness, not power, that undermines organizational effectiveness" (Tjosvold, 1984, p. 72). That depends, of course, on the type of power being talked about and how it is operated. Steers (1991, pp. 491–492) captures the essence of the power question: "People are often uncomfortable discussing the topic of power, which implies that somehow they see the exercise of power as unseemly. On the contrary, the question is not whether power tactics are or are not ethical; rather, the question is *which* tactics are appropriate and which are not. The use of power in groups and companies is a fact of organizational life that all employees must accept. In doing so, however, all employees have a right to know that the exercise of power within the organization will be governed by ethical standards that prevent abuse and exploitation."

It is not the existence of power that causes problems of trust. It is how it is employed that raises ethical considerations and questions of exploitation. There is no doubt that the abuse of power contributes mightily to the problems of trust in government. For example, the recent disclosure of secret radiation tests conducted by the former Atomic Energy Commission on at least 800 unwary civilians reinforces public mistrust in government. When a group of White House aides are discovered using presidential helicopters to play golf, it is seen as an abuse of power. When the Social Security Administration pays out about $32 million in bonuses to employees, including nearly $10,000 to an executive who had been on the job less than three months, cynicism is bound to increase.

But these are only the higher-profile cases. Inside public agencies, power is misused daily. Cronies are promoted who do not deserve to be. Raises are given to people who have not earned them. People are harassed, intimidated, and coerced in countless ways every day by bosses who misuse their authority. These are what a friend once characterized as the "little murders" in organizational life. While they do not get the attention of the more notorious cases, they too are fatal for trust.

Types of Power

There are various sources and types of power in organizations. Any deliberation about power typically begins with French and Raven's classical description of five classes of power: (1) reward, (2) coercive, (3) legitimate, (4) expert, and (5) referent (1959). Each class can help or hinder trust relations, depending upon how it is employed.

Reward Power. Reward power is based on the capacity to benefit others. For it to be effective, the target of influence must value the compensation offered. In operant learning terms, this means an authority has the ability to positively reinforce desired behavior. Rewards can be either extrinsic, such as pay, promotions, and decent working conditions, or intrinsic, such as enabling staff to control the conception and execution of their work. As has already been discussed in some detail, reward power builds trust only when it is fair, reliable, and equitable both in terms of outcomes and process.

Coercive Power. Coercive power always means threatening people in some way or using force to get things accomplished. Using coercion to control employees involves fear and intimidation, which are antithetical to trust. The higher the levels of anxiety that coercion produces, the more likely it is that individuals will engage in self-protective, low-risk behavior. They will stay downwind of trouble by keeping away from their jobs, avoiding meetings, ducking responsibility, and keeping their mouths shut. The use of fear usually gets only grudging compliance. It kills the creative zeal in people, precipitates resistance, and makes enemies.

Coercion has yet another problem in its application. It is the wrong method to get extraordinary work done in contemporary organizations. This is because the nature of work has evolved in ways that make force a constraining rather than an emancipating dynamic. What it takes these days to achieve really superior performance is freeing and synthesizing three very different technologies: machine work, craft work, and computer work. Taken together, these lead to a management method known as "smart work." It scorns force as a primary power style (Carnevale and Hummel, 1992).

Smart work is the ability to tease high performance out of very different and often competing technologies. The emergence of work teams, empowerment schemes, quality initiatives, increased employee participation and involvement, and other bottom-up, cooperative strategies are a clear reflection that top-down, auto-cratic, directive, transactional, and coercive power methods are insufficient to release the productive potential of employees. In the final analysis, coercion and the low trust that often drives it or awakens from it should always be a suspect strategy in the post-modern workplace.

Legitimate Power. Legitimate power means that the focal person being influenced recognizes the right of another individual to request compliance. It is mainly related to the position authority or status one has in an organization's hierarchy. In Weberian terms, it is rational-legal command. In other words, orders or requests are perceived as lawful because the person giving them is recognized as having the prerogative to issue them.

Respect for authority is a widely shared value in our society. Rank matters. In their families, churches, and schools people are socialized at very early ages to obey the direction they receive from their superiors. People are prepared for playing their parts or roles in an essentially bureaucratic society where hierarchy is the key mechanism of control. This norm of respect for rightful domination is assiduously maintained in organizations.

Despite this natural deference to legitimate authority, employ-ees do not always appreciate being told what to do. In the newly emerging world of work, employees increasingly expect, no matter what technology dominates their jobs, to have more supervision over their work; they want the unity of design, execution, and con-trol of how to respond to a responsibility returned to them (Carnevale, 1991). They want more hands-off management in recognition of their own hands-on skills. Even if an organizational agent has the right to tell people what to do, it is not always the necessary or right thing to do. Legitimate authority ought to be used, like coercive power, somewhat judiciously in contemporary organizations.

Authority is also a common source of suspicion in our society. Americans are decidedly schizophrenic about the use of power, even the legal kind. We are always on the lookout for the abuse or misapplication of power by people legally authorized to rule our lives. The thing about legitimate power is that it must be clearly recognized, verifiable, and called for before it will be accepted. It must be used wisely. People who primarily rely on their badges of authority to get things done are inherently less trusting and less trustworthy. It is doubtful that they can inspire high performance over the long haul in today's organizations.

Expert Power. Expert power comes from mastery in an area that is valued in an organization. This gives people credibility; others will turn to them for direction or accept their influence on a wide range of matters. It is the best example of the potency of knowhow in organizations. It is much more widely distributed than is usually appreciated. There are experts everywhere. They do everything: sweeping floors, operating technology, meeting with clients, running programs, and making policy. Experts at every level must be respected for what they know.

Long before I entered this profession, I was an expert blue-collar worker. I could throw cases of beer onto a truck faster than anyone on the shop floor. The size of containers was the secret. Sixteen-ounce cans would toss better than any bottles, especially quarts. When I worked for a prefab housing manufacturer, I could put the hardware on doors at a rate that astounded my more senior colleagues. The trick was how I spun the door on the jig. When I was in Army boot camp, I was a wonder at cleaning a floor—a true expert. My secret, which can now be revealed, was to apply rubbing alcohol after buffing. The gleam would blind you. In each case, I was valuable and respected for what I knew and had discovered on my own. To interfere with my ability to apply my knowhow would have shortchanged both me and my organization. The way to manage me, and a lot of others like me, was to make sure we had the proper tools and get out of our way.

Unlike reward, coercive, and legitimate power, which are prescribed by the organization, expert power is an individual or team characteristic that exists apart from anyone's official or formal status. Most organizations can readily identify people who have little official position power but, because of their knowhow or expertise in some area, wield considerable authority in what and how things get done. People have faith in individuals and groups who know what they are doing and mistrust those who do not. That is why knowledgeable individuals and teams must be allowed to shape how the work is performed in organizations. To deny this power to operating personnel shows a lack of faith that will be reciprocated in kind.

Referent Power. Referent power means that individuals will identify with a particular individual because of admiration for that person's personality, values, or behavior. This means employees allow themselves to be influenced because of their attraction to the personal qualities of another. They want to establish and maintain a relationship with that person. This is a charismatic kind of power and, like expert command, does not necessarily depend upon legitimate or position authority. Similar to expert power, this kind is also widely diffused throughout a work system. Referent power may arguably be the most significant of all because it ties into people's deep psychological identification, commitment, and trust of others.

Referent power has its virtues, but it also has its drawbacks. It is powerful when it inspires people to do great work, not just from a sense of duty, utilitarian exchange, or fear, but because they respect another person. If the person being admired is ethical, sensitive to subordinates' needs, and committed to high levels of organizational performance, then referent power is both ethical and constructive. If the person being revered is unabashedly ambitious, tramples upon the rights and feelings of others, disrespects the knowhow of subordinates or colleagues, and is destructive of an organization's social fabric, then trust and performance suffer. Both types of behaviors may lead to personal success and attract followers. The 1980s taught that greed and heartless careerism are rewarded and selflessness and public service denigrated. That is because ruthlessness as well as virtue are compensated in contemporary organizations. It is certain, however, that entirely self-interested power destroys trust and will ultimately become a drag on organizational performance.

The use of various bases of power has different consequences for employee behavior. Reward, coercive, and negative legitimate (threatening) power produce *compliance*; people obey out of a sense of obligation or fear, or because they expect to be rewarded. Strong commitment and enthusiasm are lacking and the potential for resistance or creating adversaries is high. Expert, referent, and positive legitimate power (focusing constructively on job performance) foster *internalization* or intrinsic motivation and lead to higher levels of performance (Kreitner and Kinicki, 1992; Steers, 1991).

When it comes to trust, two things are clear. First, since trust is dependent on a person's perception that an individual or group will be ethical, fair, and nonthreatening in situations where there is some risk or vulnerability, it is easy to see why expert, referent, and positive legitimate power have more trust-inducing properties than more threatening and directive tactics. Second, since faith in the knowledge of operating personnel is critical to an organization's success, appreciation of the widespread diffusion of expert and referent power, regardless of rank, combined with the positive and tactful use of legitimate power, also fosters greater trust.

The Need for Power

People learn to want power for different reasons. David McClelland (1970, 1975, 1976) identifies two faces of power: institutional and personal. The first helps organizations and staff to realize goals. The latter serves the needs of the power holder. Authorities motivated by institutionalized power (also known as socialized power) see it as necessary for the achievement of organizational goals. Individuals with a strong need for personal power are "power hungry" and employ it primarily for their own personal gain.

People who wield institutional power are seen by McClelland

(1975, pp. 75–78) as more effective and successful. This is because, while they believe in the importance of authority and the discipline of work, they are altruistic and consider justice and even-handed treatment above everything else. People with socialized power intentions understand power as necessary capital in organizational life. Power is the currency required to secure vital resources, to empower subordinates, and to get things done. This awareness eludes those who have personal power needs. They want power because it makes them feel important. They are stimulated by self-aggrandizement and unbridled ambition.

It is the lucky person indeed who has not confronted organizational climbers whose principal drive is to get ahead at all costs, to control others, to be at the center of things because it validates them as individuals, and whose ethical calculus considers only how their decisions benefit their own careers. People who are in it for themselves will sell out their friends, trade on their relationships, compromise organizational interests for their own advantage, dishonor agreements, use information to leverage situations to favor themselves, and engage in other unethical behaviors to get ahead. It would be easy to dismiss these behaviors as unhappy examples of individual moral failure, but they are much more than that. They reflect the fact that many organizations encourage and reward such activities and allow people to operate without ethical boundaries. In either case, the implications for organizational trust are clear.

Politics

Politics involves the use of power to get something done in social systems; it is about who gets what, when, and how (Lasswell, 1936). Power and politics are closely related concepts. Politics, like power, is not necessarily bad and it is certainly widespread in organizations. Politics is caused by uncertainty and opportunity. Politics is played when there are scarce or unclaimed resources, problems in intergroup relations, disagreement on ends and the means to achieve them. Politics is a way to serve ambition. Politics also emerges where the conditions surrounding decisions are ambiguous, where there is unresolved prior conflict, personality disputes, unequal distribution of power, introduction of new technology, or change. Individuals, groups, coalitions, and networks in organizations have agendas designed to win power and influence; they are always poised to enhance or protect their self-interests. Traditional conflict is a close cousin of politics. It arises whenever different interests collide. But today, high performance requires something different.

Politics is not just a negative force. In its original meaning, politics is recognition of divergent interests and a means for allowing people to resolve their differences through consultation and negotiation, rather than resorting to autocratic rule. It is a way of formulating jointly conceived social problems and of solving them without creating a coercive form of social order. Since organizations are simultaneously systems of collaboration and competition, political competency is a precious commodity if social cohesion is to be maintained. The issue with politics is exactly like the one with power. It is not whether politics will exist, but what kind of politics will exist.

Politics is intertwined with ethical questions and issues related to trust:

Ethical, High-Trust Actions

Forming coalitions

Avoiding petty disputes

Keeping promises

Appealing to ideals and values

Telling the truth

Being civil

Willingness to accommodate, compromise, and collaborate

Keeping conflict functional

Not personalizing disputes

Allowing people to save face

Unethical, Low-Trust Actions

Machiavellian behavior

Concealing intentions

Insincerity

Blaming others

Personalizing conflict

Spreading rumors about people

Harboring grudges

Promoting zero-sum legitimacy

Engaging in character assassination

Lying

To be ethical, politics must satisfy the interests of the organization and its staff, respect the entitlement of affected parties, and ensure both distributive and procedural justice for employees and clients. The ethical, high-trust behaviors outlined here are straightforward. These behaviors are politics, a word that suggests diplomatic, discreet, judicious, fair, and thoughtful conduct. That may sound naive, but it is the essence of constructive politics and a rare asset in modern organizations. If there were more of these kinds of behaviors, there would be more trust, less defensiveness, increased learning, and better performance in public institutions.

A second set of actions constitutes a certain deportment that is decidedly uncivil and breeds mistrust. These unethical, low-trust behaviors are also outlined in the list above. One thing these impolitic behaviors have in common is that they are motivated by a negative, low-trust view of how the world operates. Some people say they really do not *want* to behave in these ways, they are just being practical and realistic. What they fail to recognize is that adopting these methods becomes self-fulfilling. They help cause the very unethical climate people complain about. At heart they share the dark and suspicious view of human nature that underpins the low-trust political model. Their actions create an undertone in organizations that is absolutely corrosive. People choose the kind of politics they get.

Conflict

Conflict is a process of opposition, antagonistic interaction, and confrontation between individuals and groups. As with power and politics, how it is handled influences feelings of trust in modern settings. Because of the inevitability of both power and politics, conflict is predictable in organizations. Classical organizational theorists, however, tended to view it as peculiar and intolerable. After all, it upset the presumed equilibrium of well-designed and well-managed work systems and they attributed it to unnatural human or engineering failures.

Conflict can be functional, with positive effects, or it may be dysfunctional and reduce organizational effectiveness. The challenge is not to avoid conflict or deny its existence, but to maintain it at just the right level and in a fashion that promotes, rather than impairs, trust relations.

There are several advantages to conflict in organizations:

- It can reduce social tensions and facilitate communication within and between groups.

- It helps to sustain a certain level of necessary stimulation in organizations that keeps people thinking, being creative, or innovative as they search for rationales to support their positions or to counter arguments raised by other parties. It is particularly helpful in combating groupthink and other forms of excessive conformity that handicap group decision processes.

- It is a way to get feedback from other individuals and groups about one's perceptions, expectations, and behaviors.

- It helps to create and strengthen a sense of identity and purpose in individuals, teams, and entire organizations as differences and boundaries are clarified.

- It counters lethargy, apathetic compliance, and similar pathologies.

- It often forces out in the open issues that have been buried but desperately require attention.

- It encourages introspective, self-evaluative, and critical thinking.

- It provides opportunities for learning.

In short, conflict can help get at the truth of work situations. But there can be too much conflict in organizations. When that is the case, common interests are not recognized, communications become restricted and distorted, opponents are stereotyped as differences become exaggerated, and trust is impaired (Brown, 1983).

Too little conflict is also symptomatic of low trust. When there is not enough conflict, differences are not recognized or they are denied. There is pressure to agree; disagreement is suppressed or driven underground. Contrary views are undiscussable. Because decisions are based on insufficient or the wrong data, performance is impaired (Brown, 1983).

There are a number of ways to handle dysfunctional conflict that help build trust. First, conflict can be reduced by giving people joint assignments, or what are known as superordinate goals. No one individual can achieve the objective alone, and everyone has something at stake in the successful completion of the task. Trust is not automatically enhanced in these situations, but it is probable that communication will increase and have the effect of encouraging differences to be explored. One of the first things that happens when individuals and groups are at odds is that they may stop communicating. They withdraw from one another and conceal their activities and intentions. It often becomes a measure of loyalty, in conflict situations, not to be caught talking to the other side. Experienced mediators and negotiators know that getting disputants talking and keeping them at it is key to reducing conflict and reaching agreements.

Second, direct confrontation and bargaining can increase trust and reduce conflict. However, this depends on a number of contingencies, the most crucial of which is the style that is adopted. The negotiations cannot be "win-lose" or "distributive," which is very adversarial and inimical to trust. Integrative, "win-win," collaborative, principled, or problem-solving negotiations are what is needed. This method is based on openness, mutuality, and trust (Walton and McKersie, 1965; Fischer and Ury, 1981)

Third, the use of third parties can help reduce conflict and elevate levels of trust. This can take the form of any number of activities or interventions commonly associated with organizational development (OD). In addition to anything and everything already mentioned, this could include job enrichment and redesign, management by objectives, sociotechnical interventions, team-building exercises, sensitivity training, process consultation, grid OD, among many others (Blake and Mouton, 1985; French and Bell, 1984). The strength of OD is that it is participatory and democratic. Trust is a variable of central concern and requisite condition for success for OD practitioners. There is nothing inherently wrong with conflict in organizations, if it is treated as symptomatic of larger, deeper problems that can be constructively handled. It would be more worrisome not to have any conflict at all.

Given everything we know about people and organizations, the absence of conflict would be unnatural. That is particularly true in public organizations where there are an abundance of diverse work groups, ambiguous goals, equally unclear indicators of performance, and sharp differences in values surrounding the policy process. Public organizations are "Madisonian systems" where conflict is intentionally built into governance systems at all levels (Rainey, 1991).

Trust is influenced by the interaction of power, politics, and conflict in organizations. The important point is that the mere presence of these factors is not unusual or predictive of low trust. These dynamics are a fact of organizational life. They are useful and important processes that help people and organizations function effectively. When it comes to trust, what counts is what kinds of power, politics, and conflict organizations experience and how they choose to deal with these challenges. If they are managed in moral and ethical ways, these issues present as much opportunity as threat.

PART THREE

Liberating Public Organizations: Transcending the Bureaucratic Machine

9

Reinventing Training for a New Learning Paradigm

Since it is imperative to build trust into critical work processes such as leadership, motivation, communication, and the like, then it also makes sense that the learning model, the basis on which knowledge is acquired in organizations, needs to be redesigned to match the underlying ideas represented by these methods. Of all the means required to institutionalize trust and achievement, none is more important than authorizing employees to have some room to think critically, learn on their own, and use what they know. If you trust people, you make them stronger by building their competence. An organization cannot talk about empowerment and learning without investing in the capabilities of people. Low-trust organizations do train people, but they do it in a way that ensures that people follow standards and refrain from asking hard questions about the way things are done. People should not trust organizations unwilling to build their skills.

Organizations that learn fast, survive longer. They serve their clients and customers better and they are superior places to work. Almost everyone agrees that learning is the key ingredient of the high-performing organization. How does trust influence learning in organizations?

What follows goes beyond the customary call for more conventional training to improve the skill base of organizations. It is, rather, a summons for the application of a radically different learning theory at work. It details why the present behaviorist model of knowledge acquisition is increasingly outdated, or at the very least, restricted in what it can contribute to trust and high performance. It must be complemented by a fresh design, a high-trust paradigm that features *critical reflection* as its principal objective.

Much more is required these days to raise both trust and success in organizations than training in the latest production or service techniques. What is demanded is entrusting people to think critically about personal and organizational changes necessary for superior performance. It means trusting people to learn how and when to abandon ineffective habitual, programmed responses to job problems. This self-reflective model calls for fresh competencies, more active roles for learners, and greater investment in developing human capabilities. Unlike what passes for human resources development in most organizations these days, it is more than superficially empowering.

The Changing World of Work

There is widespread agreement that America is facing a revolution at work. At the heart of this transformation is the recognition that competitive advantage depends upon having able employees who know how to exploit fresh technologies, adapt to changing conditions, produce quality as well as quantity, and function effectively in new forms of work organizations that are flexible, team-oriented, and decidedly less bureaucratic.

A flood of research has recently appeared scrutinizing and criticizing America's readiness to address its human capital requirements. What is being called for is greater investment in, commitment to, and utilization of people's skills. Moreover, work organizations are properly reconceptualized as learning environments that must be managed in a different way (Johnston and Packer, 1987).

The reason why learning is so vital in contemporary organizations is that operating environments are less and less predictable and defy programmed response. People need to rapidly capture the meaning of experience and synthesize and translate it into usable knowhow. There are very few proven formulas any more. Those that exist have a short shelf life. People need to be able to think and constantly ask questions about the wisdom of what they, and their organizations, are doing.

Agility, adaptability, and speed are important personal and organizational qualities in the modern world. People need more than knowledge for the short term. They must know how to learn over the long haul. They need to be both effective individual performers and contributing team members. They must appreciate the measurable and the concrete, but they must also be able to interpret the unforeseen and trust their intuition about what feels right in a particular situation. They must accept less and inquire more. In today's world, people must discover, interpret, and solve problems on their own. The world does not serve up well-defined, neat puzzles like those found in the typical management training seminar or college classroom. To survive in today's workplace, "higher level learning" is dictated where central norms, frames of reference, and basic assumptions undergo constant trial (Fiol and Lyles, 1985).

The Quality of Human Capital in Government

Society cannot prosper without a competent public service. Government plays a tripartite role in the economy: producer of public goods and services, regulator of private enterprise, and complimentary asset to private production. This is not only the foundation of a free economy but essential to the maintenance of democratic institutions and the quality of life of the citizenry (A. P. Carnevale and D. G. Carnevale, 1993).

Public employment, by the late 1980s, accounted for more than 17 million people: 3 million federal workers, 4 million state government staff, and over 10 million local government employees (Shafritz, Riccucci, Rosenbloom, and Hyde, 1992, p. 177). It matters that public employees have the necessary competencies to fulfill their important roles in the economy and society. All the carefully crafted public policies and program implementation strategies in the world are worthless if employees do not have the requisite abilities to do their jobs.

Government work has always been knowledge-intensive. According to the Hudson Institute (1988), federal workers, for instance, are twice as likely to hold professional, technical, and managerial jobs as private employees. Thirty-one percent of all nonpostal employees possess at least a bachelor's degree, up from approximately 25 percent in 1976 (U.S. Office of Technology Assessment, 1988). It is anticipated that work in the national government will continue to evolve along these lines in the future, requiring more and more skilled personnel to fill its ranks (McGregor, 1988).

At the same time that the private sector became passionately interested in supply-side problems about the quality of the American workforce, similar concerns started to be evident in the public sector. It was felt that there was a serious erosion in the quality of the human capital base in government just as there was in industry (Levine, 1986). The situation was expected to worsen because of certain demographic trends, such as an aging and more diverse labor force, and slower growth in the labor supply. These dynamics were interpreted to mean that the workplace at the turn of the century would be populated by employees with obsolescent, weak, or no useful competencies at all.

In a special report prepared against this backdrop by the Hudson Institute (1988) for the U.S. Office of Personnel Management, the anxiety over workforce readiness was captured in an admonition: "For years, many Federal agencies have been able to hire and retain highly-educated, highly-skilled workforces. . . . But as labor markets become tighter during the early 1990s, hiring qualified workers will become much more difficult. Unless steps are taken now to address the problem, the average qualifications and competence of many segments of the Federal workforce will deteriorate, perhaps so much as to impair the ability of some agencies to function" (Hudson Institute, 1988, p. 29).

A year after the publication of the Hudson Institute report, another was produced by the National Commission on the Public Service, a private, nonprofit group headed by former Federal Reserve Board chairman Paul Volcker. It echoed all of the familiar themes and made the harsh prediction that "America will soon be left with a government of the mediocre, locked into careers of last resort or waiting for a chance to move on to other jobs" (National Commission on the Public Service, 1989).

In other words, the public service was going to end up with the "best of the worst" for its staff. These warnings were obviously alarming because of the recognition that nothing extraordinary gets done in public organizations without competent people and that government could expect to have to produce more with fewer employees in the future.

The Power of Human Capital

Sixty percent of competitive advantage in modern organizations comes from advances in intelligence. Stated differently, the major share of what it takes to realize personal and institutional success depends on learning, especially the experiential kind (A. P. Carnevale, 1991). This underscores that human capital—the knowledge, skills, and reasoning abilities of staff—is the decisive ingredient in the recipe for individual and organizational accomplishment.

The recognition of the value of employee knowhow has always been understood to some degree in work organizations, but many traditional managers believed that labor was a cost rather than an asset and suspected that employees could be trouble if they knew too much. Therefore, organizations tended to design themselves so that people were interchangeable and what they had to know to do their jobs was easily controlled or transferable to replacements. The more people knew or had to know to do the organization's work made them more valuable and therefore more costly. As a result, knowledge was something that was managed very carefully.

In classical economics, employees are seen as liabilities as opposed to wealth like buildings, land, and finances. They are labor costs to be minimized. They are a drag on the bottom line. From the classical perspective, what counts most about people in the production process is how many there are of them, not what they know.

Following World War II, however, the traditional outlook began to change with the rise of quantitative economics. People were puzzled about why American national income grew at a faster rate than the combined traditional inputs used to explain economic productivity. In a pioneering speech to the American Economic Association in 1960, Theodore Shultz provided the answer: the increase in skills of workers was the principal reason that made the economy prosper. In his view, education and other forms of human capital investment increased output by generating new ideas and methods, equipping employees to handle and make innovations in forms of production, and improving the connections between producers and consumers (Salamon, 1991, pp. 3–4). The idea was introduced that, in the modern age, human knowledge is the critical technology.

The Traditional Behavioristic Paradigm

Typically, creating or improving employee knowledge is done through training on the job. This training is ordinarily narrow in scope and designed to teach the requirements of specialized tasks that support constricted, low-discretion work. The goal is to make people efficient at what they already do, ensure dependable role behavior, and smooth out all operational friction in the organizational machine. Training methods are centered in the behavioristic paradigm, which operates as follows:

- It is behaviorally oriented with performance outcomes that can be observed, quantified, and criterion-referenced.
- Personal and work-related development are separated.
- The organizational ideal for which training is designed is a well-functioning machine with clear, hierarchical lines of authority, jobs that do not overlap, and rational systems of delegation and control.
- Training is designed to meets needs of individuals, not groups.
- Learning is designed on a "deficit" model that measures individuals against standard, expert-driven norms.
- Problem solving emphasizes objectivity, rationality, and step-by-step procedures.
- Training typically consists of classroom-based, formal group activities.
- Trainers focus on "pure" learning problems, with support provided to the organization to manipulate the environment to sustain outcomes (Marsick, 1988, p. 188).

Traditional training is mechanistic, lower-level learning that aims to help people repeat past behaviors and detect and correct mistakes against a set of previously established standards. It is not concerned with developing long-term capacity, but short-term performance. Much more training is done in organizations than development, especially for nonmanagerial personnel. The prevailing approach is task-oriented problem solving or instrumental learning. It teaches people to do predetermined things rather than think in a fundamental way about the strategies or tactics being used in the first place. It is bureaucratic, functionalist, and supportive of a model of work that is fast disappearing in America. It is limiting, rather than emancipating. It is low trust because it does not let people build their own theories about what is going on and how work ought to be performed (Marsick, 1990).

Training for High Performance

There are tremendous differences between traditional and high-performance work organizations and these distinctions have profound implications for the skills necessary to engender individual and organizational effectiveness.

In the traditional organization, survival depends on emphasizing efficiency, high-volume production, and cost over quality. Most job roles are specialized and boring. Hierarchy reigns; level after level of structure separates people from each other, presenting problems for communication, coordination, flexibility, and rapid response to operating contingencies. Superior knowledge is assumed to exist up the line, and the more crucial decisions are made at the top of the organizational pyramid. Improvements in goods and services are produced by a limited few. Occasional training is used to teach specific job-related skills to improve immediate performance (Competitiveness Policy Council, 1993).

What is needed in traditional operations are people who have good basic skills, who can read and follow instructions, possess decent communication and computation faculties, obey the rules, bring problems to the attention of their immediate superiors, not waste material, meet established standards, work within set tolerances, do their jobs at predetermined levels of speed, and basically get along with people. A respectable work ethic is also required, and a willingness to conform. These abilities are not inconsequential and should not be underestimated. As everyone who works knows, they are not in great supply. They do, however, represent lower-level kinds of competencies. They would be considered indispensable though minimal skills in the high-performing organization. Much more is required to get really outstanding achievement in a work system.

The high-performance organization competes on the basis of quality and faster time cycles. Its production is based on multiskilled work teams; its organizational design reduces hierarchy and enhances open communications throughout. Authority and responsibility are pushed down the line to personnel who have greater autonomy to make decisions about work arrangements. There is more employee participation, and continuous learning rather than intermittent training is emphasized. "Reciprocal commitment," based on mutual trust between the organization and the employee, is a major objective. The development of a more functionally democratic workplace featuring "robust collaboration" is a principal goal. If there is one key central organizing idea, it is that "the human resource strategy is linked with technology strategy" where the worker "gives wisdom to the machine" (Competitiveness Quality Council, 1993, pp. 49–57). These criteria require uncommon skills.

The high-performing organization demands broader, deeper, and more substantial mastery to support its operations. Employees must anticipate problems, not just react to them. They need grounding in the three Rs, but they also require strong interpersonal, learning, and problem-solving skills. They need to know not just the basics of communication, but also how to understand different kinds of communication styles within and between cultures. They need to be able to listen, not just hear. They need to be resourceful, creative, and adaptable. They must motivate themselves, set goals, fit in, handle both the task and process features of teamwork, negotiate effectively, and share leadership (Carnevale, Gainer, and Meltzer, 1990).

The new skill set is required for all workers, not just those at the point of production or service delivery. And the internal role of executives is no longer just to give orders but to effectively manage themselves and the learning process.

There is evidence that government organizations are getting the message. For instance, a recent report on executive and management development listed several competencies required for high performance in the federal government (U.S. Office of Personnel Management, 1990):

1. Ability to tolerate and work in situations of ambiguity, uncertainty, and constant change.

2. Facility to form partnerships, to work participatively, and to collaborate effectively with people.

3. A sensitivity to changing technology.

4. Negotiation skills.

5. A demonstrated commitment to the development of other people's competencies.

In other reports on the necessary skills for high performance in public organizations, the story is always the same. People need the basics like reading, writing, and interpersonal skills, but also the capacity to handle technological change, appreciate the essential nature of work systems, communicate exceptionally well to translate between knowledge domains, and work effectively with diverse individuals and teams (U. S. Department of Labor, 1991; Advisory Committee on Federal Workforce Quality Assessment, 1992). Most of all, people need to know how to learn and reason on their own.

Critical Self-Reflection

Critical self-reflection is "a process of testing the justification or validity of taken-for-granted premises" (Mezirow, 1990, p. 354) or "bringing one's assumptions, premises, criteria, and schemata into consciousness and vigorously critiquing them" (Mezirow, 1985, p. 25). It means getting below the surface of problems, beyond what superficially appears to be simple cause and effect relations between events, and making radical changes in how people confront their reality (Argyris and Schon, 1978). It is, in its own way, subversive of established power relations because it puts people much more in control of themselves and the truth of their work. This is especially valuable in the public sector.

Public work is different from that found in factory settings; it requires a good measure of critical self-reflection. This is because much of what is done in the public service directly involves human interaction, where problem finding and clarification are always at issue. The public employee has traditionally been guided in how to handle clients by excessive formalisms such as job rules and regulations, but the actual work has always been as much an art as anything else. A good deal of judgment is required to do it well.

This is experienced-based knowledge in action, what Schon (1978) labels "reflection-in-action." It is simultaneously created and applied during the encounter between bureaucrats and those they serve. "Many factors enter into the judgment required to do good work; too many for prior managerial calculation. It follows that the only reason that quality can be realized is because enlightened management leaves the worker enough time and space to make necessary deductions as to what he or she is actually confronting and discretion to adjust, as interpretation demands, to make the encounter a success" (Carnevale and Hummel, 1993, p. 14).

What is being described here is critical self-reflection and the social construction of reality. The managerial decision to permit it to happen could also be interpreted as empowerment. Lately that term *empowerment* has often been used too casually; it does not automatically equate with critical self-reflection or the freedom to decipher and engage events on one's own terms. The question that does not get asked enough is, empowered to do what?

All the management improvement schemes have loudly espoused a commitment to empowering employees. All have aimed to tap into and release the force of what employees have learned from their experience—their knowhow. The oft-cited claim is that knowledge is power and lots of it is supposedly being made legitimate throughout contemporary public organizations by one or another of these new management programs. Theoretically, critical thinking is being invited.

Unfortunately, simply because these management innovations call for participation and empowerment down the line does not mean that they demand any measure of critical reasoning. Most of what people are empowered to do with their occupational knowledge is narrowly confined to the achievement of instrumental goals. That is why instrumental, behavioristic learning still dominates work organizations. The fact remains that few public employees have much real command, either by themselves or in teams, to freely translate the meaning of their experiences and alter the fundamental processes of how their work is done. Most public staff are not really psychologically empowered at all, despite all the recent boosterism and hoopla. In many cases, there is only the attempt to integrate employees into the existing system of authority by extending a modest measure of "relative worker autonomy" designed to deal with job alienation and low trust arising out of the use of traditional command methods (Edwards, 1979; Hearn, 1988).

Power decides knowledge, not the other way around (Carnevale and Hummel, 1993). Employees know this, and that is why many are so reluctant to buy into so-called empowering change strategies. They have been burned too often. They are skeptical that they are really going to be allowed to check out their own and their organization's operating assumptions and significantly alter "the way things are done around here."

The Demand-Side Connection

Learning is vital but it cannot alone improve the effectiveness of individuals and organizations. The model of learning and the nature of work processes employed in organizations must operate in concert with one another to ensure high performance. This fact is recognized by a recent task force on federal workforce quality: "A highly qualified workforce will not *alone* be sufficient to guarantee quality outcomes; work environment, work systems and processes, leadership, customer expectations, and other elements are critical. . . . Workforce quality [is] the result of how an organization manages its inputs and outcomes through its various organizational processes" (Advisory Committee on Federal Workforce Quality Assessment, 1992, pp. 4, 17).

What is being argued here is the importance of the demand side of the human capital equation. If we look only at the problem of supply, then the solution to human capital problems centers on education, recruitment, and training. Supply-side thinking moves people away from the *types of jobs* being created and *how employers structure work processes* (Mishel and Teixeira, 1991). The immediate work context has a lot to do with developing human capital, and no discussion of upskilling or empowering workforces can ignore it.

The excellence of an organization's leadership, the nature of the reward and incentive structure, opportunities to participate, open communication, and how power is handled all interact and influence learning outcomes just as they do trust. Organizations are systems. The more trust is embedded within them, the more likely it is that there will be opportunities for self-directed learning and critical self-reflection of the kind that leads to outstanding performance. If the operating context is low trust, it is probable that lower-level formal learning will dominate because it enhances control and does not disturb the status quo—especially established power relations.

Developing Human Capital in Government

Historically, human resources development (HRD) has not been a high priority in the public sector. Of all the personnel processes in government, training and development have been the most neglected. While there have been some encouraging signs, the federal government still spends less of its total payroll on HRD than progressive domestic firms, which invest considerably more on their human assets. Public agencies have been rightly criticized for not having strategic plans for training and development activities and not connecting them to long-range organizational goals (National Commission on the Public Service, 1989). Some observers feel that, in the recent past, government has been busy helping the private sector address its human capital needs while ignoring its own (Katz, 1990; McGregor, 1988). This is not entirely the result of a lack of vision or awareness that employee knowledge matters. There are several obstacles in the public sector that obstruct human capital development.

First, the public sector faces the paradox that, while upskilling employees and expanding their discretion may lead to higher levels of performance, they also raise issues of accountability and responsiveness among members of the public who fear increased scope of action among unelected bureaucrats. The public has a fundamental mistrust of government officials, and for many people, empowering bureaucrats does not have an intuitive appeal.

Second, some of the politicians who have to appropriate the funds to invest in human capital development have no real interest in public employee excellence and even fear it for ideological reasons (Heilemann, 1990). They do not want government to get better; they make more political capital ridiculing it. Their posturing is helped by the fact that many members of the public see government in a way that serves their low-trust assumptions. People fear and mistrust government as either a dangerous beast bent on taking over every aspect of their lives or a bumbling idiot incapable of doing anything right no matter what—or both. These suspicious feelings make any investment strategy extremely difficult.

Third, the lack of adequate resources for training and development is compounded by the fact that HRD is often considered "soft." That issue arises in all sectors but is particularly vexing in the public domain. In the private sector, there are efforts to measure the rate of return on human capital investment and the worth of human assets. That undertaking is helped along by the fact that business has a bottom line that makes such accounting doable though complex. In government, on the other hand, it is much more challenging to assess return on any investment, given that public institutions tend to be rightly preoccupied by process concerns as much as outcomes. Moreover, there are conflicting values on what government should be doing in the first place, which makes assessments about the wisdom underlying any expenditure more difficult to justify. If these were not enough, public enterprises often produce intangible products that defy calculation (Kee and Black, 1985; Downs and Larkey, 1986).

Fourth, upgrading human capital and seeing the payoffs are not short-term undertakings. Organizations, both public and private, are not very good at thinking strategically over the long haul or showing much patience in waiting for results. One of the major causes of the failures of most innovative management strategies over the years is that they were quick-fix designs, and when anticipated gains were not immediately evident, they were abandoned. The same thing happens when it comes to human resources development. Further, this usual problem is exacerbated by the fact that much of the leadership atop public organizations is made up of political appointees who have very short time horizons. They are pushed away from reforming or strengthening internal work processes like human capital development in favor of attending to their external political roles (Rainey, 1991).

Fifth, the goal of improving employee skills is to enrich the quality of products and services to the public. The theory is that the better the services become, the more trust, faith, and confidence the taxpayers will have in government. It is no doubt hoped that will put an end to, or at least reduce, the level of bureaucrat bashing prevalent in society. The problem is that the majority of people who have encounters with government are already pleased by such experiences—they just do not generalize from them (Katz, Gutek, Kahn, and Barton, 1975). It is tough to encourage more investment in cultivating the abilities and discretion of public employees when the results are much less promising than in the private sector in terms of customer satisfaction (Swiss, 1992).

Finally, at the heart of all strategies to upgrade public human capital is trust in the potential of public employees to make greater contributions to organizational performance. There is confidence shown in what staff can do with what they know. There is faith they can learn and use their new skills responsibly. A sixth obstacle to realizing these assumptions is that civil service systems tend to be designed on a basis of mistrust and managed accordingly. A huge obstacle to building both trust and human capabilities in public organizations is the way human resource management systems are operated. Many are in dire need of a major overhaul.

10

Revitalizing Personnel Systems

It is vital that the components of an organization's human resources management (HRM) program mutually support the development of a high-trust work system. Progress is being made along this line at the federal level of government. Congress is considering legislation to improve government performance, there is a commitment to "reinvent" personnel practices, and many agencies are already deeply engaged with total quality management. However, as observed by the National Academy of Public Administration (1993, p. vii), "While these initiatives are laudable, no new approach to government will work if the reformers build on a wobbly base of attitudes of distrust, actions which devalue the work force and cumbersome systems which impede innovation, discourage risktaking, and promote inefficiencies."

The very foundation upon which human resources administration is built needs to be recast in the public sector. That means

This chapter is adapted from D. G. Carnevale, "The Learning Support Model: Personnel Policy Beyond the Traditional Model." *American Review of Public Administration*, March 1992, *22*, 19–36.

all the standard aspects of HRM—organizational arrangements, primary roles, job design methods, compensation strategies, decision styles, attitudes toward learning, and labor relations—must strategically align with and reinforce trust-building practices to achieve higher levels of learning and performance (Ingraham and Rosenbloom, 1990; Hyde, 1992).

This chapter focuses upon the U.S. civil service to illustrate and compare two HRM doctrines and their potential for creating trust. The first is the intensely bureaucratic, low-trust traditional model that dominates most public organizations. The second is the learning support model, which is better positioned to address the requirements of the emerging world of work.

The argument is simple. Human capital is not a strategic asset if its potential is inhibited by antiquated personnel structures. The challenge in today's work institutions is straightforward. Trust and high performance cannot be produced unless there is an empowered, high-caliber workforce utilizing state-of-the-art labor processes. Among other things, this means that conventional HRM methods must make some changes:

- Adjust their focus from individual jobs to organizationwide needs.
- Ensure that their operations are less regulatory.
- Learn to promote labor-management cooperation.
- Promote employee involvement.
- Trust agency authorities and, indeed, line managers to have more control over their personnel decisions.

The Operating Context

The future world of work is upon us; production and service are much different from the type that flourished in the smokestack and assembly-line age (Toffler, 1990; Zuboff, 1988). Technological, demographic, political, social, legal, and economic pressures are forcing modifications in how work institutions and their HRM functions operate.

Organizations as open systems are made up of interdependent parts; they cannot survive if they lack the capacity to respond to the contingencies found in their internal and external operating domains. In other words, there needs to be a good match between what constituencies require and what organizations deliver. How well an organization responds to stakeholder demands depends upon how well its structure, technology, and human resources are integrated and mutually reinforcing. The problem is that the organization and activities of public human resources management are still engineered to respond to a private low trust manufacturing model pioneered during the early 1900s. Despite dramatically changing environmental circumstances, traditional approaches persist and spread.

Structural configurations and human resource practices designed to support production-related trends in the early part of this century are clearly not suitable to confront the wave of the future. A more fluid and flexible conception of form and practice is necessary to cope with the new realities.

Human resources administration, in the modern age, cannot afford to be based upon the low-trust assumptions that guided its development over the years. There is simply too much at stake. Far from being a quiet backwater of administration, as it is so often depicted, human resources management is a dynamic and contentious field where conflicts over values, methods, and objectives are common. The practice of personnel is constantly battered by change and the insistent demands of various interests. How personnel specialists handle these highly contentious and stressful concerns has serious consequences for public support for government operations, the quality of working life of staff, and organizational performance.

The Traditional Model

Public employees are confronted with a paradox. They face high public expectations about performance while saddled with work practices that impair their ability to respond. As noted in a report on the state of human resources management in the federal sector: "While the public expects more and better government, workers are burdened with rigid and cumbersome tools that seriously undermine their capacity for efficient and timely action. Administrative systems for obtaining and accounting for monies, purchasing needed resources, and managing human resources are control oriented, centrally designed, and often work against instilling accountability at the point of performance" (National Academy of Public Administration, 1993, p. vii).

This dilemma is all too familiar to line managers and employees in government. This traditional paradigm is almost obsessively rule driven and is loathe to recognize the role that competing values play in administration. It worries more about preventing bad things from happening than helping good things to occur. It has a "one size fits all" mentality and has demonstrated limited capacity for innovation. It was designed to function like a machine, where rationality reigns and intangibles are suspect. It cannot produce quality because it was not designed to achieve it. It was engineered to assure equitable treatment of citizens, stiff-arm politicians, avoid corruption, and maximize the bureaucratic values of regularity, predictability, and impersonality.

The traditional model emerged at the turn of the century. Its initial features were the product of ideas from several sources:

1. The Pendleton Act, designed to correct the worst abuses of spoils by introducing a modest merit system administered by an independent civil service commission.

2. The politics-administration dichotomy, which encouraged the idea that administration should be buffered from politics.

3. The scientific management movement and its underlying premise that "one best way" to perform work could be discovered.

4. The closed-system implications of the "principles school" of public administration, which argued that rules of management existed and could be learned and successfully applied, notwithstanding the contingencies of an organization's internal and external environment.

The conflux of these beliefs generally conformed to bureaucratic organizational precepts and conditioned the nature of HRM systems.

Personnel systems that arose from these origins had an excessive policing mentality, compelled managers to find ways to get the work done in spite of the established personnel rules, made it difficult to reward performance, protected the incompetent, was unresponsive to executive leadership, excluded women and minorities from meaningful participation in the bureaucracy, and fostered paternalism during a period when public employee collective bargaining was coming of age. Finally, underwritten by the "privilege doctrine," the system was unilateral and sometimes arbitrary with respect to individual rights.

Widely shared perceptions of system failure led to what was thought to be major reform of the traditional model in 1978. This reform has proved to be disappointing and the public service continues to be seen in "crisis" (Levine, 1986; Levine and Kleeman, 1986). What is required now is an examination of the system's fundamental, underlying assumptions and a significant overhaul of its parameters. This does not mean that the public service should abandon its merit principles, which were restated and codified in 1978. Merit principles enjoy the widespread support of federal workers and the general public. The system that exists to implement them does not. In fact, the procedural thicket that constricts these principles has overwhelmed program managers.

A recent study summarized the current state of affairs: "Merit cannot mean, as one would assume from examining the system, excessive constraint and blind obedience to a nearly unintelligible maze of procedure. No manager or personnel director can work consistently or effectively in a system defined by over 6,000 pages of rules and regulations. One hundred years of accumulated rules and regulations are the baggage of merit. They do not clarify and define; they obscure. The current system essentially assumes that public managers must be coerced into meritorious behavior; there is no presumption that, left to their own skills and conscience, members of the federal service will nonetheless pursue quality and effective service" (Ingraham and Rosenbloom, 1990, p. 40).

The system remains rigid, overly regulated, coercive, and low trust. What is needed is a form of human resource administration that responds to the new performance requirements represented in postindustrial work, protects merit principles, liberates line managers from the excessive constraints of the present system, frees employees to have more direct control over their working knowledge, and is decidedly higher trust in its premises about people.

The Learning Support Model

Postindustrial society demands more of its workers, and organizations have responded in new ways. The recent emergence of quality as a dominant performance standard is one example of response to those challenges. Quality presumes products and services have attributes other than their gross number. Quality is just one of several new performance criteria used to evaluate the performance of modern institutions. The others, which have extended interest beyond efficiency, economy, and productivity, are variety, customization, convenience, and timeliness (Carnevale, 1991).

These precepts represent high performance. They do not operate independent of one another; they are part of an organic whole. They require employees to have the necessary flexibility to apply the full range of their competencies and skills on the job. Knowledge work, the distinctive signature of the emerging workplace, requires a shift from human resource practices characteristic of bureaucratic hierarchies to more collegial systems driven by the need to share information (Zuboff, 1988; Kanter, 1989).

The learning support model responds to the features of informed organizations. It understands work from the inside out and encourages the participation of employees. It respects hands-on knowledge and emphasizes learning. It thrives on open communications and the sharing of information. It eschews narrowly defined jobs and rewards group performance as well as individual knowledge of the work. It compensates workers fairly for what they know, not just what they do.

The primary goal of the personnel department within this framework is to empower employees who work on the front lines in public agencies. In other words, the learning support model places a premium on participation and employee development. It does not view government as a single operation but as a federation of several "industries" with varying operating domains that demand flexible and tailored human resource strategies. It envisions personnel departments as R&D enterprises, housing consultants on tap to support quality initiatives throughout the agency. Agencies are given considerable latitude to design personnel systems that address their legitimate needs. There is a strong conviction that, in most cases, federal managers would uphold merit if left more on their own. There is no presumption that people cannot be trusted.

The Two Models Counterpoised

What follows is a detailed comparison of the two models across a set of important personnel functions. The features of each are presented in stark contrast to one another. Such a method is a useful heuristic device but, as you are no doubt aware, HRM does not lend itself to such a neat bifurcation in practice.

Preferred Organizational Arrangement

There have been two basic approaches for organizing the personnel function in government. The first, the commission format, is administered by an independent civil service commission. The second model, the executive personnel system, places control of personnel administration largely in the hands of the chief executive of the government (Hays and Reeves, 1984). With the passage of the Civil Service Reform Act (CSRA) of 1978, the national system moved toward the executive model; the act abolished the Civil Service Commission and created the Office of Personnel Management (OPM). This structural reform increased the responsiveness of human resources administration to executive leadership. As a result, the personnel function was less isolated from the day-to-day work of government.

A crucial structural issue is the degree to which line agencies are allowed to exercise control over their own personnel operations. Historically, the federal personnel system has favored centralization. In the government's mass production hierarchy, agency autonomy was sacrificed in the pursuit of a cohesive, integrated merit system that protected merit principles by relying on uniform rules and procedures created and closely monitored by central personnel officials. Government was viewed as a single industry, and achieving symmetry in personnel practice among the various agencies was a major goal. This view dominated despite the fact that national public employment is really a composite of several "industries" such as education, social services, transportation, public safety, environment, and housing, among others. The strategy of institutionalizing a common, across-the-board personnel system ignores valid human resources needs that arise in the unique operating domains among agencies.

Another result of the CSRA, therefore, was the delegation of more authority for personnel activities to the agencies. Some of the specific activities that have been delegated are (1) greater direct hiring authority, (2) some ability to modify or waive qualification standards for in-service placements, (3) authority to pay higher rates to certain occupations in certain areas without prior OPM approval, (4) and allowing managers to participate more in the classification process. Most federal departments seem pleased with these and other initiatives granting them greater independence because they are expressions of faith and confidence in their motivations and competencies (U.S. Merit Systems Protection Board, 1989).

Despite the apparent shift to more decentralized forms at the top of government, the results of a recent study reveal that, when it comes to their own operations, agencies do not always practice what they have long preached about decentralization. Whereas "83 percent of respondents believe that delegation of authorities from OPM to agency personnel offices can lead to improved personnel management, only 60 percent believe the same is true when it comes to delegating authority from agency personnel offices to line managers" (U.S. Merit Systems Protection Board, 1989, p. 10). Ingraham and Rosenbloom (1990, p. 39) comment that this "inability—or unwillingness—of central personnel to trust and train other personnel in their own agencies is damning evidence of the problems with merit today."

The learning support model demands the devolution of as much personnel authority as possible away from central personnel departments into the hands of line managers. It is what Nigro (1990) calls the "personnel by managers" model. In more familiar terms, it is the "let managers manage" standard. That ought to be more broadly reconceptualized as the "let people do their work" criterion. After all, managers and their subordinates are together ultimately responsible for putting out the work. It is they who have the most to gain from innovations that spark quality. It is they who are evaluated for system outputs in terms of what they deliver to internal and external customers. All staff require some breathing room to act, experiment, and innovate. They must be trusted enough to do their jobs.

Control is really illusory anyway. What is usually being regulated is paperwork. People build careers taking in each other's administrative laundry while the real work of organizations suffers.

Roles

Personnel administration performs a number of roles in organizations (Bohlander, White, and Wolfe, 1983):

1. Policy initiation: proposing new policies or revisions of existing policy to deal with recurring problems.
2. Advice: advising line managers with questions about employee relations or work design.
3. Service: recruiting, training, assisting in the administration of labor contracts.
4. Control: making sure that line departments conform with established personnel rules and regulations.

In government, and everywhere else for that matter, personnel specialists have spent far too much of their time with the procedural elements of the system and minimal time in research and development activities, and have relied heavily on control. All of this was done without sufficiently broad input from agency managers and employees affected by their decisions (National Academy of Public Administration, 1993).

As authority shifts downward from central personnel agencies to operating unit personnel, a new framework emerges; it permits personnel departments to emphasize their advising and service roles when requested by the agencies or line managers. Ideas on how to improve system operations will be bottom up rather than top down as personnel specialists begin to trust the hands-on knowledge of line managers and their subordinates. Stated another way, the role of the personnel administrator will change from ensuring compliance with work rules to consultation with those who actually do the work (Nalbandian, 1981).

Understanding Work

The traditional personnel paradigm promotes the idea of knowledge about work from the outside in. The most common example is job analysis and classification, which rationalizes work and underpins several personnel practices such as recruitment, testing, performance appraisal, and training. As practiced in support of the mass production hierarchy, it has claimed scientific status based on its ability to know about jobs by focusing on those aspects that can be observed, gauged, and valued. It, quite simply, tends to trust what it can measure. Through its techniques, the labor process supposedly "yields up its secrets," is systematized and quantified if possible (Zuboff, 1981, pp. 41–42). The fact is that no matter how much of a job is researched and measured externally, work processes are fundamentally private affairs between the person doing it and the object being transformed. Important aspects of every job are beyond the reach of outside observers.

This approach to job analysis has been called pseudoscience (Elliott, 1985). At the very least, it is fair to say that this tack has its limits. One thing learned in the study of organizations, and especially personnel, is that strict rationality misses a lot. For example, how job functions are evaluated is ultimately very subjective. The idea that jobs in complex organizations can be appreciated from a distance, standardized, and reduced to a series of simple tasks is misplaced. Attempts to be ever more exact in drawing distinctions between jobs have led to endless problems.

Modern work is rapidly becoming knowledge work, what some have termed "smart work." It does not hold its shape for long. It is constantly changing. Moreover, knowledge of a job rests on the judgment of the person actually doing it. That is what is meant by the term "inside out." Even then, there are limits to the extent to which the essence of work can be translated into technical terms of the sort sought by job analysts. These realities necessitate adjustments in patterns of job analysis and design away from narrow, rigid classification schemes to broader, more flexible systems. At the heart of the change is greater respect given to the job knowledge of those who actually do the work.

Job analysis will continue to be an important part of personnel administration because the courts have made it so and because organizations must have a rational basis upon which to identify position requirements for the purposes of recruitment, selection, promotion, compensation, training, discipline, and so on. The question is not whether to do job analysis, but how to do it.

One of the central problems in personnel administration is that job designers, analyzers, and classifiers do not pay sufficient attention to people who do the work. As a former labor relations specialist, I can recall countless personnel appeals where the decisions of personnel job experts were overturned because their "desk audits" were cursory and out of touch with the reality of the job being performed. Job analysis must be rational, logical, and systematic. However, it need not be a unilateral process owned by the personnel administrators. Involving jobholders in the analysis will improve the process.

Compensation

The comparability of public compensation—pay and benefits—with private employers is a continuing problem. The current view in the federal sector is that compensation, in both direct and indirect terms, is not adequate to recruit, retain, and motivate employees (National Commission on the Public Service, 1989). This perspective was validated in a recent study conducted by the U.S. Merit Systems Protection Board (May, 1990), which found that compensation and related advancement issues were the most important reasons employees gave for leaving government service.

Progress has been made in reforming federal compensation practices, at least on paper, with the passage of the Federal Employees Pay Comparability Act of 1990. Creating workable pay-for-performance systems, expanding locality pay, ensuring comparable worth, and improving health care benefits, among other things, are also receiving more attention. The problem is that, even when changes are promised, they are not delivered.

Typically, alterations in compensation practices are held up by freezes, delays, and other devices by presidents and the Congress. Many federal employees do not trust that they will receive what they have been promised and are rightly demoralized by always being the first, and often the only, employees in the nation making wage and benefit sacrifices for the good of the economy or for the purposes of deficit reduction.

In addition to problems of equity and sufficiency of compensation practices, alternatives to traditional approaches on how to reward people need examination. Foremost among these is "pay for knowledge," a philosophy linked to new methods of job design that emphasize employee growth, development, and potential contribution.

Pay for knowledge is different from traditional pay systems, where salary is related to the worth of a specific job that an employee actually performs. In a pay-for-knowledge system, employees are compensated for the "number, kind, and depth of skills they develop" whether or not they use them all the time (Lawler and Ledford, 1984, p. 6). According to Walton (1985), traditional pay systems are appropriate for high-control, mass production modes of operation, whereas pay for knowledge is fitting for team-oriented and uncertain work environments where the number of skills and competencies a person possesses is crucial. In these cases, employees have a bank of skills at the ready that can be used when called upon. These skill reserves are worth a lot to modern organizations and merit additional compensation.

There is a problem, though, in getting organizations to invest in upskilling employees, particularly when the competencies being developed are not being immediately used. The whole process of skill development assumes the staff member will be around in the future to apply the acquired proficiencies when needed. Employees are free to leave organizations any time they choose. Therefore, employers have legitimate doubts when they are asked to pick up a tab to make people more valuable elsewhere. It is natural that they mistrust the notion that they should spend scarce resources on development activities that may never benefit their agencies. If pay for knowledge is ever to work, there has to be some confidence that organizations will realize a fair return on their investment.

Another major area needing improvement in compensation administration is the focus on individual pay. Current incentive systems are built almost entirely on gauging how much individuals should be rewarded. Group work receives only marginal attention, even though most of what gets done in organizations is, and has always been, a direct result of how well teams or units operate. Modern organizations cannot preach the value of teamwork on the one hand and have their entire reward system operate as if group activities were not valuable. Ignoring the reality of group work erodes employee faith in organizations.

Learning

The case for organizational learning is clear, and was discussed in some detail in the previous chapter. It is worth reaffirming, however, that distinctive learning occurs at the individual, group, and organizational levels. Therefore, increasing an organization's capacity for learning entails more than just training individuals. It also means supporting team learning. As Senge (1991, p. 40) observes, "Teams, not individuals, are the fundamental learning unit in modern organizations; unless the team can learn, the organization cannot learn." Therefore, human resources management has got to take a more active role in shaping organizational culture, norms, and values in order to support an organization's overall learning capacity.

All in all, most HRM departments have a good deal of work to do to adequately address their learning support roles in organizations. There is increased attention to individual training and development, but much of that is biased toward managerial and executive development. Not enough development activity is aimed at employees on the front lines. They tend to get only trained— and they do not even get enough of that.

The National Performance Review, the foundation document for reinventing government, found that the most striking problem in federal training is the lack of career training for people on the lowest rungs of the career ladder or people without college educations. Without such training, too many employees find themselves in dead-end jobs.

Much more is needed. Supervisors must be better prepared for their changing roles in the modern organization. The training of teams in group processes requires increased attention. The nature of the dominant learning philosophy in organizations also needs rethinking. The barriers to human capital development in the public sector are formidable but they are not insurmountable.

Labor Relations

Unions exist in a big way in the public sector: teachers, police officers, firefighters, sanitation workers, social service personnel, transportation employees, and correctional officers—among others—are highly organized. Unionism in America these days should no longer conjure up images of the autoworker or the steelworker. It is the public employee who dominates the unionized landscape. In the public sector, the issue of how labor relations is conducted is meaningful for employee trust and organizational performance. As discussed previously, the role of public unions in improving organizational performance is, at best, unsettled.

The importance of labor-management relations in modern organizations cannot be overemphasized. For example, unions can facilitate or obstruct quality improvement programs. Since much of the recent effort to improve organizational performance and service delivery directly depends on employee involvement and participation, union cooperation in such ventures can be an asset.

Getting unions to cooperate is not easy, and issues of trust are the core of the problem. Industrial relations researchers have identified trust as one of the most important institutional features influencing whether or not unions will cooperate with management (Kochan, Katz, and McKersie, 1986).

Unions do not trust cooperation, and a fair number of managers are conflicted about it as well. Unions are suspicious because they have seen employee involvement programs used in union-avoidance campaigns, to extract craft knowledge before transferring it to nonunion plants, to subvert or coopt local leadership, and because it violates what some leaders see as their responsibility to be ever vigilant against "managerialism." Managers have their own reasons for cynicism. Joint ventures are seen as undercutting their authority, threatening their self-esteem, inviting employee criticisms of the way they do things, and costing them their jobs.

When management and labor cooperate, good things can happen in the public sector. An employee quality circle at the U.S. Customs Service in Houston made recommendations that improved the processing of passengers from four hundred people per hour to one thousand. At the Copyright Office in Washington, an AFSCME local participated in a quality of work life program and helped reduce turnaround time for certain copyright applications from as much as four months to two weeks. At San Francisco General Hospital, employee suggestions to use the hospice model to treat AIDS patients resulted in a 40 percent reduction in the average cost of AIDS treatment. In New York, union and state administrators established a statewide labor-management committee to convert unemployment insurance offices into one-stop community service offices (Applebaum and Batt, 1994).

Human resource departments customarily have responsibility for the conduct of all employee relations programs, including those dealing with unions. What can they do to overcome these obstacles to trust and cooperation? The first thing is to accept the legitimacy of the union. It is difficult to trust and cooperate with someone who does not think you ought to be around. Management must forswear efforts to undermine the union. That means, for instance, that they cannot try to dominate quality improvement teams.

Second, extensive consultation is called for where information is widely shared between the parties. Third, the legal rights of both groups must be respected. Fourth, agreements must be honored. Fifth, and most important, the groups must learn how to work collaboratively. Taken together, these actions are a good down payment on increasing trust, cooperation, and organizational performance.

Knowing How Is Not the Problem

There is no doubt that organizations cannot expect either trust or high performance while relying on outdated personnel management systems. However, the staying power of the traditional model should not be underestimated. One reason is that it embodies well-understood personnel techniques (Nigro, 1990). In short, we know how to do it. What is not sufficiently recognized is that the learning support model comes with a technology as well (Golembiewski, 1985). We know how to do it too.

We already know how to enrich jobs. We are aware that it is illegal and destructive to discriminate against people. We grasp how to involve employees at work. We know how to talk straight. We understand enough about job analysis not to take it all too seriously. We ought to comprehend by now that there is no optimal method to evaluate performance independent of how people are treated during the process. Decentralizing operations is no mystery. We know how to deal with change and how to cooperate with unions. We comprehend enough about voice-giving procedures to enable employees to directly express how they feel about their working conditions. We surely have learned enough about the practice of human resources management to know it is not hard science.

In short, it is folly to argue that the traditional approach ought to endure just because we have mastered its techniques. We have the knowledge to substantially change human resources administration in the public sector so it is better integrated and used as a strategic asset to improve performance. We know how to make the change, but so far have lacked the will.

Conclusion: Realizing the Vision of High-Trust Public Organizations

People want to trust. It is a powerful and natural desire. They want to have faith in the social institutions that govern their lives. This is particularly true on the job. As we know, however, more and more employees have learned to be wary when they head off to work. Many, in fact, are downright cynical; they are disappointed, disillusioned, and have lost faith in their organizations. Their hopes and expectations have been mismanaged.

The destruction of the psychological contract between organizations and their members creates defensive work cultures characterized by mutual suspicion and mistrust. In these circumstances, people expend a great deal of their energy trying to protect themselves. They are anxious and worried about their futures. They are also bitter, angry, and unwilling to fully commit to organizational purposes. Their frustration is debilitating and ruins organization performance.

The Knowledge Advantage

The core performance advantage in every organization is how the capacity of the knowledge base is established and used. In low-trust work cultures, the knowledge foundation is systematically repressed and destroyed. Fear-induced defensive routines spontaneously ensue, and people cannot learn or work effectively. In today's operating environment, the result is poisonous.

How work is performed in today's world continues to evolve away from fear-inducing authoritarian control. The management of individual technical competencies is no longer paramount. Today, routine work is replaced by knowledge work, smart work, which requires the integration of different kinds of knowhow and the creation of multiskilled work teams. A new model of workplace management is summoned that places less emphasis on command and control skills and more on facilitating, synthesizing, coaching, political, and teaching competencies. The social and psychological interpretation of the meaning of information rather than just following the rules is what matters most in the contemporary organization. It is a much more subtle and fragile undertaking. To reveal the truth of work, flexible and emancipatory job arrangements are required rather than old-fashioned regulation strategies. These generative mechanisms build trust, reduce anxiety, and promote learning.

In the modern age, the job of institutional authorities is not to elicit obedience but to create the conditions where people can discover through their own experiences how work wants to be performed. Work structures and processes that obscure or repress what is really going on end up misrepresenting reality. When the truth of the work situation is denied, organizations rely on insufficient data, the wrong information, or distorted intelligence. They may think they have a good grasp on things, but they are fooling themselves. They have smothered what is actually happening by denying employees a chance to be involved, to learn, to express their opinions, and control their work. No organization can prosper in the long run when it systematically undercuts the power of its own people—its knowledge base.

This concluding chapter builds on earlier discussions and shows how trust can be reconstructed in work organizations. The basic argument is that trust grows best in nonbureaucratic environments—more specifically, in democratic administrative systems.

Trust and Democratic Administration

Organizations are societies and the spirit of trust helps bind them together. However, trust will not blossom in just any kind of social order. Trust requires for its unfolding a particular kind of government that involves certain expectations, mutual obligations, and a special combination of rights and duties between people. In high-trust work cultures, staff can count on certain experiences:

1. Voice, or freedom of speech.
2. Opportunities to be effectively involved in decisions.
3. Enforceable constitutional protections when they are evaluated, rewarded, and especially when they are punished.
4. Guarantees against the abuse of power.
5. Expectations that politics and conflict will be ethically managed.
6. Possibilities for critically self-reflective learning and individual self-development.

It is as much a political philosophy as it is an administrative doctrine. We can think of it as representing the fundamental norms of democratic administration. Democracy means direct involvement and participation in determining work conditions and organizational policies. The concern is for both individual responsibility and organizational well-being. Democracy is a moral ideal. As Wall (1991, p. 135) notes, democracy, whatever else it may mean, is self-determination; it is the empowerment of others to make their own decisions; it is the absence of coercion. To advocate noncoercion is to advance regard for others; it is the moral point of view.

Trust flourishes in democratic climates. In these surroundings, people feel safer and better able to grasp the truth of themselves and their work. They are capable of overcoming the learned powerlessness, trained incapacities, and the stultifying effects of hierarchical control structures.

Democracy is founded upon trust. There is a measure of faith and confidence in the nature and potential of people. It is acknowledged that people are not angels, but systems of governance can be constructed that try to take advantage of their best, not their worst, capacities.

In democratic work structures:

1. Power is dispersed.
2. Authority is diffuse.
3. There is less surveillance, fear, and use of force.
4. Political bargaining, compromise, accommodation, and collaboration are used rather than authoritative command to resolve conflict.
5. People have an opportunity to define their own interests.
6. The conception and execution of work routines are reintegrated.
7. There is open dialogue.
8. Teamwork is valued.
9. Resources are widely distributed.
10. Critical thinking is invited; employees are liberated to more fully confront the demands of the work as they understand it.

An organization serves democratic values to the extent that it reflects five interacting factors (Bernstein, 1980, cited in Golembiewski, 1985, p. 199):

1. Participation by all relevant organization members in decision making, either directly or through representatives.
2. Frequent feedback of the results of organizational performance, not only in terms of information but also in terms of variable rewards keyed to performance.
3. Sharing of both management-level information and expertise throughout the organization.

4. Guarantees of individual rights, which correspond essentially to the basic political liberties that are so commonly
   unavailable to individuals in both public and business organizations.

5. The availability of appeal or recourse in cases of intractable
   disputes, decision units of which will at least in part be composed of peers.

We can characterize these as participation, free speech, consti-
tutionalism, and opportunities for individual self-development
through sharing of information. They are at once fundamental
determinants of trust, democracy, and learning.

The question of democratic administration, or the necessity and
consequences of democracy *in* administration, is enduring (Waldo,
1952; Bennis, 1966; Marini, 1971; Golembiewski, 1985). The fact
that authoritarian work cultures are dominant in our society is a
major paradox. Perhaps the best-known explanation comes from
Waldo (1948, p. 75): "Autocracy at work is the unavoidable price
for democracy after hours."

However, in the case of administration, the incongruity of using
authoritarian means to achieve democratic ends has received considerable notice and is not without its critics. A number of voices
have persistently raised sharp questions about whether this is the
best way to organize and manage public institutions.

There is a direct relationship between administrative practices
and political theory. Administrative methods are political theories
in action. In public administration, the dominant ideology has been
autocratic. If organizations can be understood as systems for making decisions (Simon, 1946), then hierarchy, or unilateralism, is
the prevalent philosophy (Harmon, 1981). Despite the argument
that democratic states must be democratically administered (Levi-
tan, 1943), public administration in America has ironically fea-
tured low-trust, authoritarian control structures as its commanding
form.

How Much Democracy?

Issues of democracy in administration raise broader concerns of bureaucratic accountability and control. Mosher (1969, p. 374) provides the classic description of the dilemma:

> I would point out that *democracy in administration*, if carried to the full, raises a logical dilemma in its relation to *political* democracy. All public organizations are presumed to have been established to operate for public purposes—i.e., for purposes of the people. They are authorized, legitimized, empowered, and usually supported by authorities outside of themselves for broad purposes initially determined outside of themselves. To what extent, then, should "insiders," the officers and employees, be enabled to modify their purposes, their organizational arrangements, and their means of support? It is entirely possible that internal administrative democracy might run counter to the principles and objectives of political democracy in which organizations of government are viewed as instruments for public purposes [original emphasis].

These are reasonable questions. Golembiewski (1985, p. 225) responds by calling for exploration of a middle ground between autocracy on the one hand and direct democracy on the other. Rosenbloom (1971) also calls for more balance in response to Mosher's concern. The fact is that no symmetry presently exists and the administrative system is decidedly out of equilibrium in favor of bureaucratic rule. The center of gravity in public organizations can shift significantly toward the defensible interests of employees without destroying the democratic basis of the government. Adjustments are made constantly in the organizational arrangements of public agencies to facilitate policy implementation and for other instrumental purposes. Some accommodation to increase the democratic nature of the public workplace is as worthy a justification and very much in order.

The worry about how democracy within administration threatens the very foundations of the larger political system reminds me of the original arguments used to prevent collective bargaining for public employees. It was claimed that the introduction of negotiations in the public realm would offend the idea of sovereignty, that government would somehow be diminished if it went about the grubby business of executing contracts with people. Of course, government made bargains all the time. It just was not terribly interested in doing that with its own employees. The sovereignty argument was specious and ultimately discredited. The real problem had to do with sharing power. The same is true in this case.

How democracy in administration coexists with popular democracy is a fair, thoughtful, and important issue. However, to do nothing to restore some measure of balance in the authority equation between individuals and organizations will do nothing to help resolve the problem of trust. It also denies the truth that alterations are made all the time in how government is structured and operates.

Refusing to make changes in the bureaucratic model will not just frustrate employee trust, but will also subvert government effectiveness. More direct involvement, participation, open communication, enriched jobs, flatter hierarchies, decentralization, teamwork, and empowered front-line staff are at the heart of present quality initiatives and reinventing government plans, which purport to better serve the public interest or the common good. These same dynamics and intentions have been at the core of Theory Y, MBO, quality circles, Theory Z, and every other management innovation that has arisen during the past fifty years.

There is a huge amount of empirical evidence indicating that these tactics combine to have positive effects on employee attitudes and behaviors, as well as organizational accomplishment. The reason, once again, is that these methods allow employees a greater measure of control over their jobs and take advantage of the experienced-based learning. Given that learning is the critical technology at work today, it is imperative that bureaucratic designs recede or yield to some reasonable degree, not just to make employees less cynical but to realize higher levels of organizational performance.

Breaking Down Bureaucracy

There has always been some belief, or at least hope, that excessively bureaucratic organizations that dissipate trust and the full productive power of employees could not long endure. One reason is that they violate democratic norms or represent the wrong values (Marini, 1971; Denhardt, 1993). Another is that they are generally dysfunctional and actually impair organizational effectiveness (Thayer, 1973; Hummel, 1987b). They are also seen as not suitable designs for the emerging world of work where the unfettered flow of information and the creation of learning systems are prized (Zuboff, 1988; Toffler, 1990; Carnevale, 1991). Finally, they are not viewed as particularly healthy places for adults to develop and, therefore, ought to be changed (Argyris, 1957; Golembiewski, 1985).

It is evident, despite these well-founded critiques, that bureaucracy not only perseveres but continues to dominate the organizational landscape. It is no wonder that trust is in such trouble, given the values of the bureaucratic ideal and the behaviors it encourages and rewards. How might the situation be changed?

Overarching Principles

Work organizations are communities, and linking democratic values in society to those found in the workplace is crucial for building trust. What follows is a discussion of problems and prospects for changing the low-trust, antidemocratic internal logic or mindset that dominates contemporary public organizations.

Change the Labor Relations Model

Much of what passes for bureaucratic reform continues to be top-down initiatives controlled by higher authorities in organizations.

The central idea is that workers down the line are to be empowered to take on more responsibility for work activities. This is accomplished primarily through various forms of involvement or participation programs.

As discussed earlier, the role of unions gets scant notice in the latest schemes to transform public organizations. This book is about trust, and the way unions have been handled in the movement to reform bureaucracy is decidedly low trust. The proposition here is simple, although some may find it somewhat radical. It is that there needs to be greater involvement of unions in all efforts to transform public organizations into high-trust, high-performing work systems. Many employee involvement techniques echo some of the worst aspects of the human relations movement of the 1930s, and that must stop. Many are parallel structures for change that do not threaten or change the distribution of power, and that must cease. In the end, high-trust organizations are not based on managerial unilateralism or paternalism. If organizational authorities trust the knowhow, motivation, and commitment of employees, then institutionalize workable labor-management processes and learn to cooperate for mutual gain.

Strengthen Supervision

All of the activities related to building trust in organizations are typically performed by supervisors. That is where the rubber meets the road in public organizations. First-level supervision is the face of management, and it is especially important in creating the quality of working life of employees. It is the supervisor who hires, rewards, fires, suspends, demotes, assigns work, promotes, trains, evaluates performance, and facilitates communication and involvement. The question is, how well prepared is supervision in government to handle its important responsibilities of creating high-trust work cultures?

Since supervision accounts for or explains the major variance in worker attitudes on the job, it is imperative that supervisory selection and training be given much higher priority than it has up to now. Supervision at every level is a difficult role and it merits more support, if trust is to be strengthened in organizations. In my study of public employees in Florida (Carnevale, 1988), for example, I found that supervisors had serious problems in trusting their organization. It is likely then that they diffused those attitudes to subordinates.

How much do employees trust supervisors in your organization? How much do supervisors themselves trust your organization? What are the attitudes of supervisors in your organization toward more democratic forms of supervision? What kinds of training and development programs are available to supervisors in your organization? What do they feature? Answering these questions is helpful in getting at issues of trust in any organization.

Do Not Create a Two-Tier Employment System

An obvious problem for trust in contemporary organizations is the perception that people at the top do not care much about or look out for the interests of people at the bottom. A recent report by the Labor and Commerce Departments (Manegold, 1994) details the development of an underclass of low-paid and unskilled workers unable to compete in the new world of work. There is a polarization of the American workforce into "haves" and "have nots." The report noted that a healthy society could not remain stable under such conditions.

Public organizations do not exist in a vacuum. They face the same issue of polarization. It is easy to understand that building trust, quality, and high performance from the bottom up will be impossible unless there is ample opportunity for everyone at work.

At the heart of greater opportunity is the need for a stronger commitment to upgrade employee skills. Trust, democracy, and opportunity depend on building greater competencies in lesser-skilled workers. Public organizations need to gauge how well they are doing when it comes to allocating training, wages, benefits, and upward mobility for everyone on the job. When an employment ghetto—a structural underclass—for low-level workers is created, it is certain that organizational trust will suffer.

An example of a problem in the making has to do with blue-collar workers in the federal government. The federal blue-collar workforce represents nearly 350,000 employees in over 300 different occupations. A 1992 Merit System Protection Board report shows that blue-collar employees have fears about losing their jobs because of downsizing. Their morale is low. They say they are treated like second-class citizens, and they do not feel fairly paid. They believe the quality of their supervisors needs to be improved, they find numerous problems with their performance appraisal process, and they want more training. Given what we know about trust formation, this is a recipe for trouble.

Stop Treating People As Disposable

Manpower Inc., with 560,000 workers, is the world's largest temporary employment agency and one of America's biggest companies. It specializes in supplying companies with qualified temporary employees. These people fill a specific need for a period of time and then are let go. They are part of a growing "disposable" workforce, one of the most significant employment trends in the United States today.

Some of these temporary workers prefer part-time job arrangements, but many have no other choice. They are the casualties of the fraying social and psychological contract in the American workplace. There are obvious advantages to employers in using people in this way. They usually do not have to pay benefits. They do not need to worry about some compliance issues and potential litigation if they have to discharge somebody. It is easier to get rid of people that are not wanted any more.

Some people who supply part-time workers feel they are doing them a favor. One commented, for instance, "We are not exploiting people. We are not setting the fees. The market is. We are matching people with demands. What would our workers be doing without us? Unemployment lines? Suicide?" (Castro, 1993, p. 46). Being a step up from suicide is progress, I suppose, but one wonders if there are not costs to organizations in terms of trust, team spirit, loyalty, commitment, and other intangibles so necessary for high performance.

It is no doubt tempting, in an era of diminishing resources, for organizations to take a low-security, low-wage, low-benefit path in employment. However, they need to take a long-term view of such practices and carefully weigh all the hidden costs to their organizations before they buy in too enthusiastically to such programs.

Think Incrementally

Bureaucratic organizations are difficult to change. They are particularly challenging to change all at once. But large-scale organizational change can be accomplished.

Organizational development (OD) is a technology, philosophy, and attitude that has been successful in transforming public organizations through a variety of planned change strategies. We can be somewhat optimistic that substantial progress can be made in reforming bureaucracy through the use of OD (Golebiewski, 1985). However, the question is whether it is realistic to expect sweeping change strategies, particularly at the deep level of trust, to be successful.

There is an alternative, known as "purpose-driven, incremental OD," that achieves breakthrough changes by focusing on a subsystem strategy. The timing and pacing of change occur in response to a strategy of "logical incrementalism" or "muddling through" (Kobrak, 1993). Like all OD models, it is democratic.

The principles of OD are also consistent with all the core ideas expressed in this book. For instance, Patten (1989, p. 3) observes that, to build better organizations, "one begins with trust, then moves to include—at a minimum—openness, authenticity, participation, democratic problem-solving, innovation, and organizational justice." This is an ambitious agenda and needs to be approached realistically. Entrenched bureaucracy cannot be swallowed whole in most cases. Small, manageable bites may be more practical for building trust.

Behave Ethically

My original study of the predictors of trust in public organizations was my dissertation, and it employed a quantitative analysis of survey data as its primary method. In the original model, extent of ethical conduct by higher-level administrators was hypothesized as a likely predictor of trust. The data analysis showed that respondents lumped ethical conduct and trust together. In other words, they saw the two constructs as representing the same thing. That presented some analytical problems for me.

The important theoretical point, however, is that trust and ethics are inseparable. They are highly related concepts. An organization cannot have one without the other. Leadership is self-serving and exploitive or it helps people grow beyond dependency. Voice is encouraged or punished. Participation is allowed or it is constrained. There is or is not some degree of organizational fairness and justice. Power, politics, conflict are handled in ethical and moral ways or they are not.

In terms of the everyday processes of organizational life, ethical conduct helps determine the climate of trust. As an overriding prescription for building trust, administrators need to take note.

Conclusion

Is trust an old-fashioned notion? Does it have a place in modern organizations? The answer is clear. Without trust, individuals and their organizations cannot function effectively. When trust is reduced, individual and organizational power drops significantly.

Trust is the bedrock of organizations because the trusting relationship has special power in dealing with the everyday problems that arise in all work situations. Trust makes it possible for people

with different responsibilities and personal agendas to interact effectively in the midst of change and stress without making every
encounter potentially explosive or requiring a formal bargain before
cooperation can ensue. More important, it eases the social interaction that leads to the exchange of essential information upon which
learning is based.

The idea that trust is rapidly fading is acknowledged. However,
mistrust and low confidence are not destiny. Different consequences
can be realized. There are organizations and parts of organizations
throughout society that enjoy high levels of trust and commitment
on the part of their employees. There are places where people actually like their jobs. There are instances where people look forward
to going off to work. They enjoy the time spent with co-workers.
They also feel that their jobs contribute meaning to their lives and
do some good for society at the same time. It is through work, any
kind of work, that people discover a lot about themselves. It is
where they can experience community, connectedness, and personal growth. Working hard can generate a good deal of positive
psychic energy. Indeed, it is true that work can be like play.

Creating high-trust work organizations is within the control of
administrators. It is the choices they make about how an organization is managed and structured that ultimately determines employee
attitudes and behaviors on the job. The more work processes express
confidence in employees, the more likely it is that they will respond
in the same spirit. Trust is a reciprocal attitude.

There is an interesting kind of physics that surrounds the
dynamic of trust. Gibb (1978, p. 238) describes four fundamental
propositions that capture the dynamics of how trust operates at work:

1. Personal behavior produces *trust*; role or depersonalized
   behavior produces defense.
2. Authentic *openness* produces integration of living process;
   covert strategy produces counter strategy and circumven-
   tion.
3. Internal *realization* results in high productivity; persuasion
   produces resistance and disintegration.

4. Independence produces synergy; control produces dependency/rebellion.

The message is clear. Trust and high performance are impossible if the organization deals with employees just in terms of their work roles, puts up defenses that impair free expression, uses manipulative methods to motivate workers to do what it wants, and attempts to control everything and everyone.

Trust is not a "soft" factor in organizational life. It is not some kind of institutionalized smile button. The hard-headed reason trust is consequential is that people who feel secure willingly move down a path where they become better learners and contributors in an organization. On the other hand, staff who are suspicious and cynical go a different way. They become absorbed in self-protective practices. They are less likely to take risks, to speak out when it is called for, to question ideas that need examination, to participate during meetings, or take a chance that a fresh approach might be the answer to a problem. They fear speaking truth to power. Who, after all, is going to expose themselves to risk or commit to an organization that weakens their sense of efficacy or threatens their very existence? Who identifies with a system that keeps them small?

The ways to build trust have been detailed throughout this book. We know what needs to be done and we understand how to proceed. Here are a few of the more obvious prescriptions:

- Get people involved. Show confidence in what they know.
- Appeal to people's higher-order competencies.
- Aim for beyond-contract behaviors, not just simple compliance.
- Diffuse leadership. Promote self-management rather than rely on charisma.
- Open up communications and discuss the undiscussable.
- Enrich jobs and promote teamwork.
- Provide first-rate service to clients. Let people with a public service motivation act on it.

- Welcome conflict and politics and handle them in decent and ethical ways.

- Model, rather than order, the behavior expected from others. It is what is done, not what is said, that counts.

- Be fair in managing rewards and punishments. Remember that everyone is watching, and process considerations matter most in how people assess fairness.

- Accept the legitimacy of the union and promote cooperation where possible.

- Facilitate and teach more and command less. Work is changing and requires different skills.

- Promote learning, particularly the critically self-reflective kind.

- Respect the dignity in all work.

- Demonstrate respectable assumptions about people's motivations and abilities. You are likely to reap what you sow concerning your attitudes about employees.

- Develop a human resources management system that supports, rather than obstructs, what is being built.

- Keep promises and honor obligations.

- Above all else, remember that less bureaucracy is better.

These are just a few of the basic ingredients in the recipe for trust and high performance. It must be remembered that these elements work only in combination or in tandem with one another. They are part of an *integrated work system*. It does little good to implement one or two of these ideas and expect that the world is going to be turned upside down. Organizational structuring, work design, employee involvement plans, technology strategies, human capital development programs, and human resources policies have to be managed in a coherent, self-reinforcing way.

It is one thing to take a system apart to diagnose it, as we have done here. It is quite another to put it back together and manage it. Organizations are systems composed of interdependent parts. Superior organizational management calls for the integration and synthesis of disparate elements to achieve the synergy of high performance.

There is no mystery about how to build trust and achieve high performance in organizations. The prescriptions identified here are not new. Researchers in organizational theory, organizational behavior, organizational development, personnel, industrial psychology, and labor relations, for instance, have known for a long time what is called for to improve the functioning of human institutions. The problem is, as it has always been, getting people to let go of the ideology that supports the power of hierarchical control structures.

The reforms will not come as fads. Every few years it seems a trendy new idea comes along that is supposed to fix the employee alienation or commitment problem. It enjoys its brief moment of popular acclaim and then retreats into the background as a newer idea takes its place. In each case, results consistently fall short of what is promised and employees are weary of it. Worse, they are made more cynical than before. People are tired of hearing promises of involvement when the locus of power in their organizations never moves one iota. Despite the claims, it is fair to say that most American workers do not feel empowered at work. Despite the hoopla, staff everywhere are dispirited and many more are plain afraid about their futures.

There is nothing "hot" about trust. The worse thing that could happen to it is that it would ever become in vogue. Trust takes a painfully long time to build. It can be destroyed in a heartbeat. People want to trust. They have learned not to. When trust is restored, employees and their organizations have a fighting chance to find a measure of meaning at work and achieve more in the public interest. The spirit of trust is power, and it needs to be reinstitutionalized at work.

References

Adams, J. S. "Toward an Understanding of Inequality." *Journal of Abnormal and Social Psychology*, 1963. *67*, 422–463.

Adams, J. S. "Inequality in Social Exchange." In L. Berkowitz (ed.), *Advances in Experimental Social Psychology*. New York: Academic Press, 1965.

Advisory Committee on Federal Workforce Quality Assessment. *Federal Workforce Quality: Measurement and Improvement*. A Report to the U.S. Merit Systems Protection Board and the U.S. Office of Personnel Management. Washington, D.C.: Advisory Committee on Federal Workforce Quality Assessment, 1992.

Alderfer, C. P. "An Intergroup Perspective on Group Dynamics." In J. W. Lorsch (ed.), *Handbook of Organizational Behavior*. Englewood Cliffs, N.J.: Prentice-Hall, 1987.

American Arbitration Association. *Alternative Dispute Resolution in the United States: A Bibliography*. New York: American Arbitration Association, 1987.

Applebaum, E., and Batt, R. *The New American Workplace*. Ithaca, N.Y.: ILR Press, 1994.

Argyris, C. *Personality and Organization*. New York: HarperCollins, 1957.

Argyris, C. *Understanding Organizational Behavior*. Belmont, Calif.: Dorsey Press, 1960.

Argyris, C. *Knowledge for Action: A Guide to Overcoming Barriers to Organizational Change*. San Francisco: Jossey-Bass, 1993.

Argyris, C., and Shon, D. A. *Organizational Learning: A Theory of Action Perspective*. Reading, Mass.: Addison-Wesley, 1978.

Armshaw, J., Carnevale, D., and Waltuck, B. "Cooperating for Quality: Union-Management & Partnership in the U.S. Department of Labor." *Review of Public Personnel Administration*, 1993, *13*(3), 94–107.

Associated Press. "Job Stress Growing Worldwide, Report Says." *The Daily Oklahoman*, March 23, 1993a, p. 13. Associated Press. "Gas Chain Monitors Employees." *The Norman Transcript*, Aug. 13, 1993b, p. 11.

Bandura, A. *Social Foundations of Thought and Action: A Social Cognitive Theory*. Englewood Cliffs, N.J.: Prentice-Hall, 1986.

Barber, B. *The Logic and Limits of Trust*. New Brunswick, N.J.: Rutgers University Press, 1983.

Barnard, C. I. *The Functions of the Executive*. (13th anniversary ed.) Cambridge, Mass.: Harvard University Press, 1968. (Originally published 1938.)

Bass, B. M. *Leadership and Performance Beyond Expectations*. New York: Free Press, 1985.

Bendix, R. *Work and Authority in Industry*. New York: Wiley, 1963.

Bennis, W. G. *Changing Organizations*. New York: McGraw-Hill, 1966.

Bennis, W. G., and Nanus, B. *Leaders: The Strategies for Taking Charge*. New York: HarperCollins, 1985.

Berger, P. L., and Luckmann, T. *The Social Construction of Reality: A Treatise in the Sociology of Knowledge*. New York: Doubleday, 1967.

Bernstein, P. *Workplace Democratization: Its Internal Dynamics*. New Brunswick, N.J.: Transaction Books, 1980.

Bies, R. J. "The Predicament of Injustice: The Management of Moral Outrage." *Research in Organizational Behavior*, 1987, *9*, 289–319.

Blake, R. R., and Mouton, J. S. *The Managerial Grid III*. Houston: Gulf Publishing, 1985.

Blau, P. M. *Exchange and Power in Social Life*. New York: Wiley, 1964.

Bohlander, G. W., White, H. C., and Wolfe, M. N. "The Three Faces of Personnel, or, Pair Department Activities as Seen by Executives, Line Managers, and Personnel Directors." *Personnel*, 1983, *60*, 12–22.

Boss, R. W. "Trust and Managerial Problem-Solving Revisited." *Group and Organization Studies*, 1978, *3*, 331–342.

Bowman, J. S. "At Last, an Alternative to Performance Appraisal:

Total Quality Management." *Public Administration Review*, 1994, *54*(2), 129–137.

Braverman, H. *Labor and Monopoly Capital.* New York: Monthly Review Press, 1974.

Brief, A. P., and Motowidlo, S. J. "Prosocial Organizational Behaviors." *The Academy of Management Review*, Oct. 1986, *11*(4), 710–726.

Broder, D. S. "Dialogue Makes for Democracy." *Norman Transcript*, Apr. 25, 1994, p. 6.

Brown, L. D. *Managing Conflict at Organizational Interfaces.* Reading, Mass.: Addison-Wesley, 1983.

Buchholz, S., and Roth, T. *Creating the High-Performance Team.* New York: Wiley, 1987.

Bullock, A. *Hitler: A Study in Tyranny.* London: Penguin, 1962.

Burns, J. M. *Leadership.* New York: HarperCollins, 1978.

Carnevale, A. P. *America and the New Economy: How New Competitive Standards Are Radically Changing American Workplaces.* San Francisco: Jossey-Bass, 1991.

Carnevale, A. P., and Carnevale, D. G. "Public Administration and the Evolving World of Work." *Public Productivity and Management Review*, Fall 1993, *xvii*, 1–14.

Carnevale, A. P., Gainer, L. J., and Meltzer, A. S. *Workplace Basics: The Essential Skills Employers Want.* San Francisco: Jossey-Bass, 1990.

Carnevale, D. G. "A Model of Organizational Trust: A Case Study in Florida State Government." Unpublished dissertation, Florida State University, 1988.

Carnevale, D. G. "The Learning Support Model: Personnel Policy Beyond the Traditional Model." *The American Review of Public Administration*, 1992, *22*, 423–435.

Carnevale, D. G. "Root Dynamics of Alternative Dispute Resolution: An Illustrative Case in the U.S. Postal Service." *Public Administration Review*, 1993, *53*(5), 1–7.

Carnevale, D. G., and Hummel, R. P. "Managing Smart Work in the Public Sector." *Working Paper*, University of Oklahoma, Norman, Oklahoma, 1992.

Carnevale, D. G., and Hummel, R. P. "The Soul in the Machine: Quality, Power and the Future of Work." Paper presented at 54th National Training Conference, San Francisco, Calif., July 1993.

Carnevale, D. G., and Wechsler, B. "Trust in the Public Sector: Individual and Organizational Determinants." *Administration & Society*, 1992, 23(4), 471–494.

Carr, C. "Managing Self-Managed Workers." *Training & Development*, Sept. 1991, pp. 36–42.

Castro, J. "Disposable Workers." *Time*, March 29, 1993, pp. 43–47.

Chapa, J. "Rebuilding Public Trust: The Vital Role of Nonprofessional Public Servants." In F. J. Thompson (ed.), *Revitalizing State and Local Public Service: Strengthening Performance, Accountability, and Citizen Confidence*. A Publication of the National Commission on the State and Local Public Service. San Francisco: Jossey-Bass, 1993.

Church, G. "Gorezilla Zaps the System." *Time*, Sept. 13, 1993, pp. 25–28.

Cohen-Rosenthal, E., and Burton, C. *Mutual Gains*. New York: Praeger, 1987.

Committee on the Evolution of Work. *The New American Workplace: A Labor Perspective*. Washington, D.C.: AFL-CIO, Feb. 1994.

Competitiveness Policy Council. *Reports of the Subcouncils*. Washington, D.C.: Competitiveness Policy Council, March 1993.

Conger, J. A. "Theoretical Foundations of Charismatic Leadership." In J. A. Conger, R. N. Kanungo, and Associates, *Charismatic Leadership: The Elusive Factor in Organizational Effectiveness*. San Francisco: Jossey-Bass, 1988.

Dahl, R. "The Concept of Power." *Behavioral Science*, 1957, 2, 202–203.

Danzinger, J. N., and Kraemer, K. L. *People and Computers: The Impacts of Computing on End Users in Organizations*. New York: Columbia University Press, 1986.

Dasgupta, P. "Trust as a Commodity." In D. Gambetta (ed.), *Trust*. New York: Basil Blackwell, 1988.

Deal, T., and Kennedy, A. *Corporate Cultures*. Reading, Mass.: Addison-Wesley, 1982.

Deci, E. L. *Intrinsic Motivation*. New York: Plenum, 1975.

Deming, W. E. *Out of Crisis*. Boston: Cambridge Center for Advanced Engineering Study, Massachusetts Institute of Technology, 1986.

Denhardt, R. B. *Theories of Public Organization*. (2nd ed.) Belmont, Calif.: Wadsworth, 1993.

Deutsch, M. "Trust and Suspicion." *Journal of Conflict Resolution*, 1958, *11*(4), 265–279.

Deutsch, M. *The Resolution of Conflict*. New Haven, Conn.: Yale University Press, 1973.

Downs, A. *Inside Bureaucracy*. Boston: Little, Brown, 1967.

Downs, G. W., and Larkey, P. *The Search for Government Efficiency: From Hubris to Helplessness*. New York: Random House, 1986.

Dresang, D. L. *Public Personnel Management and Public Policy*. (2nd ed.) White Plains, N.Y.: Longman, 1991.

Dumaine, B. "Creating a New Company Culture." *Fortune*, Jan. 15, 1990, pp. 127–131.

Eddy, W. B. *Public Organization Behavior and Development*. Cambridge, Mass.: Winthrop Publishers, 1981.

Edwards, R. *Contested Terrain*. New York: Basic Books, 1979.

Elden, J. M. "Political Efficacy at Work: The Connection Between More Autonomous Forms of Workplace Organization and a More Participatory Politics." *The American Political Science Review*, 1981, *75*, 43–58.

Elliott, R. H. *Public Personnel Administration: A Values Perspective*. Reston, Va.: Reston Publishing Company, 1985.

Etzioni, A. *Complex Organizations*. Troy, Mo.: Holt, Rinehart, and Winston, 1961.

Farnham, A. "The Trust Gap." *Fortune*, Dec. 4, 1989, pp. 56–78.

Fiol, C. M., and Lyles, M. A. "Organizational Learning." *Academy of Management Review*, 1985, *10*(4), 803–813.

Fischer, R., and Ury, W. *Getting to Yes*. New York: Penguin Books, 1981.

Fletcher, C. "Tinker Innovator." *Tinker AFB Newsletter*, 1993.

Folger, R., and Greenberg, J. "Procedural Justice: An Interpretive Analysis of Personnel Systems." *Research in Personnel and Human Resources Management*, 1985, *3*, 141–183.

Fox, A. *Beyond Contract: Work, Power and Trust Relations*. London: Faber and Faber, 1974a.

Fox, A. *Man Management*. London: Hutchinson & Co., 1974b.

French, J.R.P., Jr., and Raven, B. "The Bases of Social Power." In D. Cartwright (ed.), *Studies in Social Power*. Ann Arbor: Institute for Social Research of the University of Michigan, 1959.

French, W. L., and Bell, C. H., Jr. *Organization Development: Behavioral Science Interventions for Organization Improvement*. (3rd ed.) Englewood Cliffs, N.J.: Prentice-Hall, 1984.

Friedlander, F. "The Primacy of Trust as a Facilitator of Further Group Accomplishment." *Journal of Applied Behavioral Science*, 1970, 6, 387–400.

Gerth, H., and Mills, C. W. (eds.). *From Max Weber: Essays in Sociology*. New York: Oxford University Press, 1946.

Gibb, J. R. "Defensive Communication." *Journal of Communication*, 1961, 11, 141–148.

Gibb, J. R. "Climate for Trust Formation." In L. Bradford, J. Gibb, and K. Benne (eds.), *T-Group Therapy and Laboratory Method: Innovation in Re-education*. New York: Wiley, 1964.

Gibb, J. R. *Trust: A New View of Personal and Organizational Development*. Los Angeles: The Guild of Tutors Press, 1978.

Gibson, J. L., Ivancevich, J. M., and Donnelly, J. H., Jr. *Organizations*. Homewood, Ill.: Irwin, 1991.

Giffin, K., and Barnes, R. E. (eds.). *Trusting Me, Trusting You*. Columbus, Ohio: Merrill, 1976.

Goins, B. "From Red Tape to Results: A Government That Works Better & Costs Less." Quoted in A. Gore (ed.), *Report of the National Performance Review*. Washington, D.C.: 1993.

Goldberg, S. B. "Grievance Mediation: Successful Alternative to Labor Arbitration." *Negotiation Journal*, 1989, 5, 9–15.

Golembiewski, R. T. *Men, Management, and Morality*. New York: McGraw-Hill, 1965.

Golembiewski, R. T. *Humanizing Public Organizations*. Mt. Airy, Md.: Lomond Publications, 1985.

Golembiewski, R. T. "OD Perspectives on High Performance: Some Good News and Some Bad News About Merit Pay." *Review of Public Personnel Administration*, 1986, 7, 9–27.

Golembiewski, R., and McConkie, M. L. "The Centrality of Interpersonal Trust in Group Processes." In C. L. Cooper (ed.), *Theories of Group Processes*. New York: Wiley, 1975.

Golembiewski, R. T., Munzenrider, F., and Stevenson, J. *Stress in Organizations: Toward a Model of Burnout*. New York: Praeger, 1986.

Goodsell, C. T. "Reinvent Government or Rediscover It?" *Public Administration Review*, 1993, 53, 85–87.

Gore, A. "From Red Tape to Results: Creating a Government That Works Better & Costs Less." *Report of the National Performance Review*. Washington, D.C.: 1993.

Gouldner, A. W. "The Norm of Reciprocity." *American Sociological Review*, Apr. 1960, *25*, 161–178.

Gray, P. "Lies, Lies, Lies." *Time*, Oct. 5, 1992, pp. 32–38.

Greenberg, J., and Folger, R. "Procedural Justice, Participation, and the Fair Process Effect in Groups and Organizations." In P. B. Paulus (ed.), *Basic Group Processes*. New York: Springer-Verlag, 1983.

Half, R. "Managing Your Career: 'How Can I Stop the Gossip?'" *Management Accounting*, Sept. 1987, p. 27.

Harmon, M. M. *Action Theory for Public Administration*. White Plains, N.Y.: Longman, 1981.

Harris, C. "Preparing for a 'Revolution'—Unionists, Managers Set to Overhaul Relations." *Federal Times*, Oct. 25, 1993, *29*, 37.

Harris, C. "More Latitude Changes Attitudes." *Federal Times*, March 21, 1994, *30*, 6, 12.

Hays, S. W., and Reeves, T. Z. *Personnel Management in the Public Sector*. Needham Heights, Mass.: Allyn & Bacon, 1984.

Hearn, F. *The Transformation of Industrial Organization: Management, Labor, and Society in the United States*. Belmont, Calif.: Wadsworth, 1988.

Heckscher, C. *The New Unionism: Employee Involvement in the Changing Corporation*. New York: Basic Books, 1988.

Heilemann, J. "Government Agencies Are a Haven for the Mediocre Because They Don't Try to Get Anybody Better." *Washington Monthly*, Dec. 1990, pp. 39–46.

Holzer, M., and Rabin, J. "Public Service: Problems, Professionalism and Policy Recommendations." *Public Productivity Review*, 1987, *43*, 3–13.

Horton, T. R., and Reid, P. C. *Beyond the Trust Gap*. Homewood, Ill.: Business One Irwin, 1991.

House, R. J., Woycke, J., and Fodor, E. M. "Charismatic and Noncharismatic Leaders: Differences in Behaviors and Effectiveness." In J. A. Conger, R. N. Kanungo, and Associates (eds.), *Charismatic Leadership: The Elusive Factor in Organizational Effectiveness*. San Francisco: Jossey-Bass, 1988.

Howell, J. P., Dorfman, P., and Kerr, S. "Moderator Variables in Leadership Research." *Academy of Management Review*, 1986, *11*, 88–102.

Hudson Institute. *Civil Service 2000*. Prepared for the U.S. Office of

Personnel Management Career Entry Group, Washington, D.C., 1988.

Hughes, K. "Whistle Blowers Wary of Special Counsel." *Federal Times*, Jan. 3, 1994a, 29(47), 4.

Hughes, K. "Managers Join Forces to Plead Their Case." *Federal Times*, Jan. 24, 1994b, 29, 50.

Hummel, R. P. "A Case for a Bio-Social Model of Charisma." Paper prepared for delivery at the 8th congress of the International Political Science Association, Munich, Aug. 31-Sept. 5, 1970.

Hummel, R. P. "Freud's Totem Theory as Complement to Max Weber's Theory of Charisma." *Psychological Reports*, 1974, 35, 683–686.

Hummel, R. P. "Behind Quality Management: What Workers and a Few Philosophers Have Always Known and How It Adds Up to Quality Management." *Organizational Dynamics*, 1987a, 16, 71–78.

Hummel, R. P. *The Bureaucratic Experience*. New York: St. Martin's Press, 1987b.

Huszczo, G. E. "The Long-Term Prospects for Joint Union-Management Worker Participation Precesses." *Workplace Topics*, AFL-CIO Department of Economic Research, 1991, 2, 13–36.

Hyde, A. C. "The Proverbs of Total Quality Management: Recharting the Path to Quality Improvement in the Public Sector." *Public Productivity & Management Review*, 1992, 16(1), 25–37.

Ifill, G. "Bill & Al's Traveling Medicine Show." *The New York Times*, national ed., Sept. 9, 1993, p. A–10.

Ingraham, P. W. "Of Pigs in Pokes and Policy Diffusion: Another Look at Pay-for-Performance." *Public Administration Review*, 1993, 53(4), 348–356.

Ingraham, P. W., and Rosenbloom, D. H. *The State of Merit in the Federal Government. An Occasional Paper Prepared for The National Commission on the Public Service*. Washington, D.C.: National Commission on the Public Service, 1990.

Janis, I. L. *Victims of Groupthink: A Psychological Study of Foreign Policy Decisions and Fiascoes*. Boston: Houghton Mifflin, 1972.

Johnston, W. B., and Packer, A. H. *Workforce 2000: Work and Workers for the 21st Century*. Indianapolis, Ind.: Hudson Institute, 1987.

Juran, J. M. *Juran on Planning for Quality*. New York: Free Press, 1988.

Kanter, D. L., and Mirvis, P. H. "Cynicism at Work." Unpublished manuscript, 1987.

Kanter, D. L., and Mirvis, P. H. *The Cynical Americans: Living and Working in an Age of Discontent and Disillusion*. San Francisco: Jossey-Bass, 1989.

Kanter, R. M. *Commitment and Community*. Cambridge, Mass.: Harvard University Press, 1972.

Kanter, R. M. *When Giants Learn to Dance*. New York: Simon & Schuster, 1989.

Katz, D. "The Motivational Basis of Organizational Behavior." *Behavioral Science*, 1964, 9, 131–146.

Katz, D., Gutek, B. A., Kahn, R. L., and Barton, E. *Bureaucratic Encounters: A Pilot Study in the Evaluation of Government Services*. Ann Arbor: Survey Research Center, Institute for Social Research, University of Michigan, 1975.

Katz, J. L. "Help Wanted." *Governing*, 1990, 4, 68–72.

Kee, J., and Black, R. "Is Excellence in the Public Sector Possible?" *Public Productivity Review*, 1985, 9, 25–34.

Kelman, S. *Making Public Policy: A Hopeful View of American Government*. Basic Series in American Government, J. Q. Wilson (ed.) New York: Basic Books 1987.

Keltner, J. *Interpersonal Speech—Communication*. Belmont, Calif.: Wadsworth, 1970.

Kerr, S. "Substitutes for Leadership: Some Implications for Organizational Design." *Organization and Administrative Sciences*, 1977, 8, 135–146.

Kerr S., and Jermier, J. M. "Substitutes for Leadership: Their Meaning and Measurement." *Organizational Behavior and Human Performance*, 1978, 22, 375–403.

Kets de Vries, M.F.R. *Leaders, Fools, and Imposters: Essays on the Psychology of Leadership*. San Francisco: Jossey-Bass, 1993.

Kobrak, P. "Toward a Broader Approach to Organization Development." *American Review of Public Administration*, Dec. 1993, 23(4), 319–341.

Kochan, T., Cutcher-Gershenfeld, J., and MacDuffie, J. P. "Employee Participation, Work Redesign, and New Technology: Implications for Public Policy in the 1990s." In *Investing in People: A Strategy to Address America's Workforce Crisis*, Commission on Workforce Quality and Labor Market Efficiency. Washington, D.C.: U.S. Department of Labor, 1989.

Kochan, T. A., Katz, H., and McKersie, R. *The Transformation of American Industrial Relations*. New York: Basic Books, 1986.

Kochan, T., Katz, H., and Mower, N. "Worker Participation and American Unions." In T. A. Kochan (ed.), *Choices Facing American Labor*. Cambridge, Mass.: MIT Press, 1985.

Kouzes, J. M., and Posner, B. Z. *The Leadership Challenge: How to Get Extraordinary Things Done in Organizations*. San Francisco: Jossey-Bass, 1987.

Kouzes, J. M., and Posner, B. Z. *Credibility: How Leaders Gain and Lose It, Why People Demand It*. San Francisco: Jossey-Bass, 1993.

Kreitner, R., and Kinicki, A. *Organizational Behavior*. (2nd ed.) Homewood, Ill.: Irwin, 1992.

Laurent, A. "Discontent Mixed with Mischief Makes Sabotage." *Federal Times*, July 1993a, 29(21), 32.

Laurent, A. "A Word of Warning for Gore's Group." *Federal Times*, July 1993b, 11.

Lawler, E. E. *Pay and Organizational Effectiveness*. New York: McGraw-Hill, 1971.

Lawler, E. E. *Pay and Organization Development*. Reading, Mass.: Addison-Wesley, 1981.

Lawler, E. E. *High-Involvement Management: Participative Strategies for Improving Organizational Performance*. San Francisco: Jossey-Bass, 1986.

Lawler, E. E., and Ledford, G. E., Jr. "Skill-Based Pay." Working paper no. 89: University of Southern California Center for Effective Organizations, 1984.

Leventhal, G. S. "What Should Be Done with Equity Theory?" In K. J. Gergen, M. S. Greenberg, and R. H. Willis (eds.), *Social Exchange: Advances in Theory and Research*. New York: Plenum, 1980.

Leventhal, G. S., Karuza, J., and Fry, W. R. "Beyond Fairness: A Theory of Allocation Preferences." In G. Mikula (ed.), *Justice and Social Interaction*. New York: Springer Verlag, 1980.

Levine, C. "The Federal Government in the Year 2000: Administrative Legacies of the Reagan Years." *Public Administration Review*, 1986, 46, 195–207.

Levine, C., and Kleeman, R. S. "The Quiet Crisis of the Civil Service: The Federal Personnel System at the Crossroads." Washington, D.C.: National Academy of Public Administration, 1986.

Levine, D. I., and Strauss, G. "Employee Participation and Involvement." In Commission on Workforce Quality and Labor Market Efficiency, *Investing in People: A Strategy to*

Address America's Workforce Crisis (Background Papers, vol. II). Washington, D.C.: U.S. Department of Labor, 1989.

Levine, D. I., and Tyson, L. "Participation, Productivity and the Firm's Environment." In A. S. Blinder (ed.), *Paying for Productivity*. Washington, D.C.: The Brookings Institution, 1990.

Levison, H. *Men, Management, and Mental Health*. Cambridge, Mass.: Harvard University Press, 1962.

Lewin, K. "Studies in Group Decision." In D. Cartwright and A. Zander (eds.), *Group Dynamics*. New York: HarperCollins, 1953.

Lewis, J., and Weigert, A. "Trust as a Social Reality." *Social Forces*, June 1985, p. 971.

Likert, R. *The Human Organization*. New York: McGraw-Hill, 1967.

Lindbloom, C. *Charisma*. Cambridge, Mass.: Basil Blackwell, 1990.

Lipset, S. M., and Schneider, W. *The Confidence Gap*. (rev. ed.) Baltimore: Johns Hopkins University Press, 1987.

Loomis, J. "Communication, the Development of Trust, and Cooperative Behavior." *Human Relations*, 1959, *12*, 305–315.

Luft, J. "The Johari Window." *Human Relations and Training News*, Jan. 1961, pp. 6–7.

Luhmann, N. *Trust and Power*. London: Wiley, 1979.

Lusche, D. "Total Quality Management at the 964th Airborne Warning and Control Squadron: A Case Study." Unpublished dissertation, The University of Oklahoma, 1994.

Luthans, F. *Organizational Behavior*. (6th ed.) New York: McGraw-Hill, 1992.

Luthans, F., Baack, D., and Taylor, L. "Organizational Commitment: Analysis of Antecedents." *Human Relations*, 1987, 4(40), 219–236.

McCall, M. W. *Power, Influence, and Authority: The Hazards of Carrying a Sword*. Technical Report no. 10. Greensboro, N.C.: Center for Creative Leadership, 1978.

McClelland, D. C. "The Two Faces of Power." *Journal of International Affairs*, 1970, 24(1), 32–41.

McClelland, D. C. *Power: The Inner Experience*. New York: Irvington, 1975.

McGregor, D. *The Human Side of Enterprise*. New York: McGraw-Hill, 1960.

McGregor, D. *The Professional Manager*. New York: McGraw-Hill, 1967.

McGregor, E. B., Jr. "The Public Sector Human Resource Puzzle:

Strategic Management of a Strategic Resource." *Public Administration Review*, 1988, 48, 941–951.

McGregor, E. B., Jr. *Strategic Management of Human Knowledge, Skills, and Abilities: Workforce Decision Making in the Postindustrial Era.* San Francisco: Jossey-Bass, 1991.

Manegold, C. "Study Warns of Growing Underclass of the Unskilled." *N.Y. Times*, June 2, 1994, A–18

Manz, C. C. "Self-Leadership: Toward an Expanded Theory of Self-Influence Processes in Organizations." *Academy of Management Review*, 1986, *11*, 585–600.

Manz, C. C., and Sims, H. P., Jr. "Searching for the 'Unleader': Organizational Member Views on Leading Self-Managed Groups." *Human Relations*, 1984, *37*(5), 409–424.

Marini, F. (ed.). *Toward a New Public Administration: The Minnowbrook Perspective.* San Francisco: Chandler, 1971.

Marrow, A., Barrows, D., and Seashore, S. *Management by Participation.* New York: HarperCollins, 1967.

Marsick, V. J. "Learning in the Workplace: The Case for Reflectivity and Critical Reflectivity." *Adult Education Quarterly*, 1988, 38(4), 187–198.

Marsick, V. J. "Action Learning and Reflection in the Workplace." In J. Mezirow and Associates (ed.), *Fostering Critical Reflection in Adulthood: A Guide to Transformative and Emancipatory Learning.* San Francisco: Jossey-Bass, 1990.

Maslow, A. *Motivation and Personality.* New York: HarperCollins, 1954.

Meyer, H. H. "The Pay for Performance Dilemma." *Organizational Dynamics*, 1975, 3(3), 39–50.

Mellinger, G. D. "Interpersonal Trust as a Factor In Communication." *Journal of Abnormal Social Psychology*, 1956, 52, 304–309.

Mezirow, J. "A Critical Theory of Adult Learning and Education." In S. O. Brookfield (ed.), *Self-Directed Learning: From Theory to Practice.* New Directions for Adult and Continuing Education, no. 25. San Francisco: Jossey-Bass, 1985.

Mezirow, J. "How Critical Reflection Triggers Transformative Learning." In J. Mezirow and Associates (eds.), *Fostering Critical Reflection in Adulthood: A Guide to Transformative and Emancipatory Learning.* San Francisco: Jossey-Bass, 1990.

Miles, R. E., and Ritchie, J. B. "Participative Management: Quality Versus Quantity." In D. A. Kolb, I. A. Rubin, and J. M.

McIntyre (eds.), *Organization Psychology*. (4th ed.) Englewood Cliffs, N.J.: Prentice-Hall, 1984.

Mishel, L., and Teixeira, R. *The Myth of the Coming Labor Shortage: Jobs, Skills, and Incomes of America's Workforce 2000*. Washington, D.C.: American Enterprise Institute, 1991.

Mishra, J., and Morrissey, M. A. "Trust in Employee/Employer Relationships: A Survey of West Michigan Managers." *Public Personnel Management*, 1990, *19*(4), 443–485.

Moore, P. *Public Personnel Management: A Contingency Approach*. Toronto: Heath, 1985.

Morgan, G. *Images of Organization*. Newbury Park, Calif.: Sage, 1986.

Mosher, F. C. *Democracy and the Public Service*. New York: Oxford University Press, 1969.

Nachmias, D. "Determinants of Trust Within the Federal Bureaucracy." In D. Rosenbloom (ed.), *Public Personnel Policy: The Politics of Civil Service*." Port Washington, N.Y.: Associated Faculty Press, 1985.

Nalbandian, J. "Performance Appraisal: If Only People Were Not Involved." *Public Administration Review*, 1981, *41*(3), 392–396.

National Academy of Public Administration. *Leading People in Change: Empowerment, Commitment, Accountability*. A Report by an Academy Panel. Washington, D.C.: National Academy of Public Administration, 1993.

National Center on Education and the Economy. *America's Choice: High Skills or Low Wages!* Rochester, N.Y.: National Commission on the Skills of the American Workforce, 1990.

National Commission on the Public Service. *Leadership for America— Rebuilding the Public Service*. Paul A. Volcker, ed. Lexington, Mass.: Lexington Books, 1989.

National Commission on the State and Local Public Service. *Hard Truths/Tough Choices: An Agenda for State and Local Reform*. Albany, N.Y.: Nelson A. Rockefeller Institute of Government, 1993.

Nigro, L. G. "Personnel for and Personnel by Public Administrators: Bridging the Gap." In N. B. Lynn and A. Wildavsky (eds.), *Public Administration: The State of the Discipline*. Chatham, N.J.: Chatham House, 1990.

Oldham, G. R., and others. "Relations Between Job Facet Comparisons and Employee Reactions." *Organizational Behavior and Human Decision Processes*, 1986, 38, 28–47.

Organ, D. W. *Organizational Citizenship Behavior: The Good Soldier Syndrome*. Lexington, Mass.: Lexington Books, 1988.

Osborne, D., and Gaebler, T. *Reinventing Government: How the Entrepreneurial Spirit Is Transforming the Public Sector*. Reading, Mass.: Addison-Wesley, 1992.

Ouchi, W. G. *Theory Z: How American Business Can Meet the Japanese Challenge*. Reading, Mass.: Addison-Wesley, 1981.

Parker, M. *Inside the Circle*. Boston: South End Press, 1985.

Patten, T. H. "Historical Perspectives on Organizational Development." In W. Sikes and others (eds.), *The Emerging Practice of Organization Development*. Alexandria, Va.: NTL Institute for Applied Behavioral Science, 1989.

Perrow, C. *Complex Organizations: A Critical Essay*. (3rd ed.) New York: HarperCollins, 1986.

Perry, J. L., and Wise, L. R. "The Motivational Bases of Public Service." *Public Administration Review*, May/June 1990, 50, 367–373.

Peters, T. J., and Waterman, R. H. *In Search of Excellence: Lessons from America's Best-Run Companies*. New York: HarperCollins, 1982.

Port, O., Carey, J., and others. *Business Week*. October 25, 1991.

Porter, L. W., and Lawler, E. E. *Managerial Attitudes and Performance*. Homewood, Ill.: Irwin, 1968.

Porter, L. W., Lawler, E. E., and Hackman, R. *Behavior in Organizations*. New York: McGraw-Hill, 1975.

Rainey, H. G. *Understanding and Managing Public Organizations*. San Francisco: Jossey-Bass, 1991.

Reich, R. *Tales of a New America*. New York: Times Books, 1987.

Richardson, C. "Progress for Whom? New Technology Unions, and Collective Bargaining." *Software and Hardhats: Technology and Workers in the 21st Century*. Washington, D.C.: Work and Technology Institute, 1992.

Rivenbark, L. "Workers' Opinion Poll Could Change Benefits." *Federal Times*, June 8, 1992, 28, 1 & 14.

Rivenbark, L. "Hate How You're Rated?" *Federal Times*, 1993, 29(20), 1 & 12.

Rivenbark, L. "Vice President Offers Survival Tips to Executives" *Federal Times*, April 11, 1994, p. 5.

Roach, S. S. "The New Majority: White Collar Jobless." *The New York Times*, March 14, 1993, p. 17.

Roelofs, H. M. *The Poverty of America: A Theoretical Interpretation.* Philadelphia: Temple University Press, 1992.

Roethlisberger, F. J., and Dickson, W. J. *Management and the Worker.* Cambridge, Mass.: Harvard University Press, 1939.

Rosenbloom, D. H. "Some Political Implications of the Drift Toward a Liberation of Federal Employees." *Public Administration Review,* 1971, *31,* 420–426.

Rotter, J. B. "A New Scale for the Measurement of Interpersonal Trust." *Journal of Personality,* 1967, *35,* 651–665.

Rowan, R. "Where Did That Rumor Come From?" *Fortune,* Aug. 13, 1979, pp. 130–34, 137.

Ryan, K. D., and Oestreich, D. K. *Driving Fear Out of the Workplace: How to Overcome the Invisible Barriers to Quality, Productivity, and Innovation.* San Francisco: Jossey-Bass, 1991.

Salamon, L. M. "Overview: Why Human Capital? Why Now?" In D. W. Hornbeck and L. M. Salamon (eds.), *Human Capital and America's Future: An Economic Strategy for the 90's.* Baltimore: Johns Hopkins University Press, 1991.

Samuelson, R. J. "The Boss as Welfare Cheat." *Newsweek,* Nov. 3, 1991, p. 55.

Schein, E. H. *Process Consultation: Its Role in Organization Development.* Reading, Mass.: Addison-Wesley, 1969.

Schein, E. H. *Organizational Psychology.* (3rd ed.) Englewood Cliffs, N.J.: Prentice-Hall, 1980.

Schein, E. H. *Organizational Culture and Leadership.* (2nd ed.) San Francisco: Jossey-Bass, 1992.

Schoen, D. A. *The Reflective Practitioner: How Professionals Think in Action.* New York: Basic Books, 1983.

Schwartz, H. S. *Narcissistic Process and Corporate Decay: The Theory of the Organizational Ideal.* New York: New York University Press, 1990.

Selznick, P. *TVA and the Grass Roots.* New York: HarperCollins, 1949.

Senge, P. M. *The Fifth Discipline: The Art and Practice of the Learning Organization.* New York: Doubleday Currency, 1990.

Senge, P. M. "The Learning Organization Made Plain." *Training and Development,* 1991, *45,* 37–44.

Shafritz, J. M., Hyde, A. C., and Rosenbloom, D. H. *Personnel Management in Government.* (4th ed.) New York: Marcel Dekker, 1986.

Shafritz, J. M., Riccucci, N. M., Rosenbloom, D. H., and Hyde, A. C.

Personnel Management in Government. (4th ed.) New York: Marcel Dekker, 1992.

Shapiro, W. "Voters' Guide: How to Tell When a Politician Is Lying." *Time*, Oct. 5, 1992, p. 38.

Sherif, M. *In Common Predicament.* Boston: Houghton Mifflin, 1966.

Simon, H. A. *Administrative Behavior.* New York: Free Press, 1948.

Steers, R. *Introduction to Organizational Behavior.* (4th ed.) New York: HarperCollins, 1991.

Stillman, R. J., II *Public Administration: Concepts and Cases.* (3rd ed.) Boston: Houghton Mifflin, 1983.

Strickland, L. H. "Surveillance and Trust." *Journal of Personality*, 1958, 26, 200–215.

"Survey of Employees: Managers Tell It Like It Is." *Federal Times*, March 1, 1993, 29(3), 16.

Swiss, J. "Adapting Total Quality Management (TQM) to Government." *Public Administration Review*, 1992, 38, 356–362.

Taylor, F. *Scientific Management.* New York: HarperCollins, 1911.

Thayer, F. E. *An End to Hierarchy! An End to Competition!* New York: New Viewpoints, 1973.

Thibaut, J., and Walker, L. *Procedural Justice: A Psychological Analysis.* Hillsdale, N.J.: Erlbaum, 1975.

Thompson, F. J. "Critical Challenge to State and Local Public Service." In F. J. Thompson (ed.), *Revitalizing State and Local Public Service: Strengthening Performance, Accountability, and Citizen Confidence.* San Francisco: Jossey-Bass, 1993.

Tjosvold, D. "The Dynamics of Positive Power." *Training and Development Journal*, June 1984, p. 72.

Toffler, A. *Power Shift: Knowledge, Wealth, and Violence at the Edge of the 21st Century.* New York: Bantam Books, 1990.

Trevino, L. K. "The Social Effects of Punishment in Organizations: A Justice Perspective." *Academy of Management Review*, Oct. 1992, 17(4), 647–676.

Tullock, G. *The Politics of Bureaucracy.* Washington, D.C.: Public Affairs Press, 1965.

U.S. Congress, Office of Technology Assessment. *Technology and The American Economic Transition: Choices for the Future.* (OTA-TET-283). Washington, D.C.: U.S. Government Printing Office, 1988.

U.S. Department of Labor. *What Work Requires of Schools.* Washington, D.C.: U.S. Department of Labor, June 1991.

U.S. Merit Systems Protection Board. *Federal Personnel Policies and Practices—Perspectives from the Workplace*. Washington, D.C.: U.S. Merit Systems Protection Board, 1987.

U.S. Merit Systems Protection Board. *Federal Personnel Management Since Civil Service Reform: A Survey of Federal Officials*. Washington, D.C.: U.S. Merit Systems Protection Board, 1989.

U.S. Merit Systems Protection Board. *Working for America: A Federal Employee Survey*. Washington, D.C.: U.S. Merit Systems Protection Board, 1990.

U.S. Merit Systems Protection Board. *Federal Blue Collar Employees: A Workforce in Transition*. Washington, D.C.: U.S. Merit Systems Protection Board, 1992.

U.S. Office of Personnel Management. *Federal Employee Attitudes*. Washington, D.C.: U.S. Office of Personnel Management, 1979.

U.S. Office of Personnel Management. *Reports of Task Force on Executive and Management Development*. Washington, D.C.: U.S. Government Printing Office, 1990.

Usery, W. J. "Some Attempts to Reduce Arbitration Costs and Delays." *Monthly Labor Review*, 1972, 95(11), 3–6.

Vaill, P. B. *Managing as a Performing Art: New Ideas for a World of Chaotic Change*. San Francisco: Jossey-Bass, 1991.

Vroom, V. H. *Work and Motivation*. New York: Wiley, 1964.

Waldo, D. *The Administrative State*. New York: Ronald Press, 1948.

Waldo, D. "Development of Theory of Democratic Administration." *American Political Science Review*, 1952, 46, 81–103.

Walker, L., Lind, E. A., and Thibaut, J. "The Relation Between Procedural and Distributive Justice." *Virginia Law Review*, 1979, 65, 1401–1420.

Walker, M. "Forest Service Cited for 'Mussling' Critics." *Federal Times*, April 25, 1994, p. 2.

Wall, B. "Assessing Ethics Theories from a Democratic Viewpoint." In J. S. Bowman (ed.), *Ethical Frontiers in Public Management: Seeking New Strategies for Resolving Ethical Dilemmas*. San Francisco: Jossey-Bass, 1991.

Walton, R. E. "From Control to Commitment in the Work Place." *Harvard Business Review*, 1985, 63, 57–74.

Walton, R. E. *Innovating to Compete: Lessons for Diffusing and Managing Change in the Workplace*. San Francisco: Jossey-Bass, 1987.

Walton, R. E., and McKersie, R. B. *A Behavioral Theory of Labor Negotiations*. New York: McGraw-Hill, 1965.

Watkins, K. E. and Marsick, V. J. *Sculpting the Learning Organization:*

       Lessons in the Art and Science of Systemic Change. San Francisco: Jossey-Bass, 1993.

Weisbord, M. R. *Productive Workplaces: Organizing and Managing for Dignity, Meaning, and Community*. San Francisco: Jossey-Bass, 1987.

Woodward, J. *Industrial Organization: Theory and Practice*. New York: Oxford University Press, 1965.

Work in America. Report of Special Task Force to the Secretary of Health, Education, and Welfare. Cambridge, Mass.: MIT Press, 1973.

Wrightsman, L. S. "Measurement of Philosophies of Human Nature." *Psychological Reports*, 1964, *14*, 743–751.

Yukl, G. A. *Leadership in Organizations*. (3rd ed.) Englewood Cliffs, N.J.: Prentice-Hall, 1994.

Zalenznik, A. "Managers and Leaders: Are They Different?" *Harvard Business Review*, 1977, *55*, 67–78.

Zand, D. E. "Trust and Managerial Problem Solving." *Administrative Science Quarterly*, 1972, *17*, 229–239.

Zuboff, S. *In the Age of the Smart Machine: The Future of Work and Power*. New York: Basic Books, 1988.

Name Index

Subject Index

W

Whistleblowers, 102
White-collar unemployment, 8
Work groups, communications in,
93–97. *See also* Communication;
Groups; Teams
Work policies: based on assumptions
about human nature, 35–37; based on
low trust, 27–28
Work roles: in bureaucratic organiza-
tions, 156; and personnel administra-
tion, 175–176; trust and, 76–78
Work systems, 68–69, 73–74
Workforce: disposable, 193–194; polar-
ization in, 192–193
Workplace: crisis of trust in, 7; manufac-
turing model for, 28–29. *See also*
Organizations

Z

Zero-sum politics, 130